Praise for *The Funding Framework-Secure Startup Funding with Confidence*

Closing a funding deal can be stressful, but *The Funding Framework* offers the perspective and strategies that make the process feel less daunting.
Kumar R. Parakala | USA National best-selling author, *Lead to Disrupt*

Finding the right investors is more than just seeking capital—it's about finding a partnership that aligns with your vision. *The Funding Framework* gave us an approach that focuses on compatibility rather than just numbers.
Tamara Nall | CEO & Founder, The Leading Niche

The book's clear, structured approach makes navigating the fund-raising process feel less intimidating. Vijay's real-world examples and straightforward advice help entrepreneurs take charge of their funding journey, no matter their experience level. As someone who has helped companies raise capital for the past 25 years, I am happy to see the topic addressed in a comprehensive book because it is a mystery to most entrepreneurs embarking upon the process.
Carl Grant III | CEO, CapitalRaise.net & Author, *How to Live the Abundant Life*

The Funding Framework offers more than just practical advice—it helps founders reframe how they think about the funding process itself. From the pitch to closing, the book highlights the emotional and strategic elements that make the difference between success and failure.
Aaron Poynton | Author, *Think Like A Black Sheep*

Vijay's book serves as a comprehensive manual that helps founders gain clarity on the entire startup journey, from securing funding to executing their vision.
Casel Burnett | Vice President, LODI, and International Bestselling Author of *No Regrets*

The Funding Framework is a game-changer for founders seeking capital. Vijay simplifies the complex world of fundraising into a strategic journey. His deep understanding of the startup ecosystem and investor psychology makes this book an indispensable guide for entrepreneurs.
Jeremy Jonker | Managing Partner, Infinity Ventures

Smart and practical fundraising advice from someone who's seen thousands of deals up close.
John Zeratsky | General Partner at Character Capital and Author of Sprint, Make Time, and Click.

THE FUNDING FRAMEWORK

SECURE STARTUP FUNDING WITH CONFIDENCE

Leaders
Press

VIJAY RAJENDRAN

Leaders
Press

ISBN **978-1-63735-339-4** (pbk)
ISBN **978-1-63735-340-0** (hcv)
ISBN **978-1-63735-338-7** (ebook)

Library of Congress Control Number: **2024915533**

Table of Contents

Foreword

There's something magical about early-stage startups.

My first encounter with startup life happened in college when a few close friends and I founded a company. Suddenly, we were building websites, navigating retail sales tax, and immersing ourselves in the real world outside academic papers. Even after that business flopped, I pursued the startup energy by joining PublicRelay, a media intelligence startup in DC. And today, as I lead the Carta Insights Team, my hope is that we can help first-time founders become second-time founders without having to go through all the messy mistakes.

However, unlocking the necessary skills, knowledge, and secrets can be troubling for many first-time founders. Many of them feel lost, or worse—they feel as though they are on the outside of some special group looking in.

Vijay's book, *The Funding Framework*, eases that trouble by simplifying the fundraising process and letting first-time founders jump inside that circle more confidently. Vijay has been an active supporter of founders around the globe, helping them grow from ambitious entrepreneurs to confident leaders. His experience, from his role at 500 Global to his work as an executive coach for startups, provides him with unique insights and experiences into the startup world.

His book provides founders with actionable insights and practical frameworks to help answer essential startup questions. Founders will encounter many different obstacles, from funding to product to self-doubt. It's key that they take a step back and try to hold on to the purpose of what they're building. At the heart of it, startups are not about what the world is now—they are about how you can impress your vision on the world and change it moving forward.

There's an inherent optimism in startups, a small band of people testing the limits of what's possible. It's why I love it so much! Whether they end up succeeding, founders are right about the impact they're about to have on the world. And I believe Vijay's book can help more people step into that journey.

Peter Walker
Head of Insights, Carta

For Sona

An Introduction to the Funding Framework

I'm an executive coach based in Silicon Valley, serving startup founders. Previously, I led portfolio value at 500 Global (also known as 500 Startups), a venture capital firm reporting $2.7 billion under management when I left in 2023. There, I formed a global team that helped startups and their founders in over eighty countries raise capital, develop connections, and create a thriving community. That first objective of raising capital uncovered many patterns about the essential and seemingly never-ending journey of startup fundraising.

Over 20 years, as an entrepreneur, investor, and advisor, I have supported hundreds of founders, and helped them on their journey to becoming CEOs. I believe that through the right coaching, we can impact the world for the better, one bold leader at a time, and improve the odds of success for the businesses that they lead. I can't coach all the people I'd like to; that's why it felt so important to write this book.

I'm excited to share with you what I've worked on with dozens of founders each year who wanted to raise capital. Often, the things they were trying to learn about fundraising and the challenges they faced were 20 percent unique to their circumstances and 80 percent consistent themes across the portfolio of startups I knew. Remarkably, this was true across geography, sectors, and areas of technology focus. That's what this book can reveal and unlock for you, the founder or owner of a growing business.

Let's dig deeper into the Funding Framework and build on crucial fundraising and relationship-building skills to launch your startup. Follow Maya's journey in the pages ahead and use this book as a travel guide, hopping to the sections that are most relevant as you navigate the startup landscape in the future.

This book contains the essentials of what you need as a startup and nothing you don't. Additionally, each chapter is intended to stand alone. Here, you will find the skills and strategies that differentiate successful fundraising efforts—from telling your story to closing a 'yes' with the right investors. Let's go!

How Maya Learned to Stop Pitching and Start Listening

In the heart of Silicon Valley, amidst the buzzing cafes and ambitious startups, we find an ambitious founder named Maya. Maya, a bright-eyed entrepreneur with a revolutionary idea, was just starting her fundraising journey. Her startup features an AI-driven analytics tool designed for small businesses that was her brainchild. It was the result of her years as an AI expert and her passion for working with different tech companies.

Maya has always believed that a good pitch was about showcasing her brilliance and the uniqueness of her idea. She had been busy the past few days, meticulously preparing every slide for her presentation and making sure they were all polished. She focused on seeing that every financial projection was optimistic yet believable. Her speech was already loaded with sophisticated words that would impress potential investors and make them nod to her startup.

The big day finally arrived, and Maya stepped into the meeting room with a venture capital firm known for funding some of the leading tech startups of the past 10 years. She was wearing her confidence and ready for any questions that would be thrown at her. Starting her pitch with enthusiasm and energy, Maya shared her journey of how she developed the idea for this analytics tool. She emphasized how her startup could help small businesses become more efficient and effective, dwelling on its features and technicalities.

The investors listened and nodded. But as minutes ticked by, their interest seemed to wane. Their eyes darted to their watches and drifted across the room. Maya tried to maintain her composure throughout the presentation, ending her speech by highlighting the potential and vision for her startup. After what she felt like a very long hour, the venture capital investors (VCs) thanked her for sharing her startup and promised to get back to her.

Days passed. Then, days turned into weeks. Maya waited, only to receive a polite and fairly vague email stating that her startup might not be the business they would support right now, but they would "be rooting for her from the sidelines." Feeling disheartened and rejected, she sought advice from a seasoned mentor and fundraiser, her friend Arya.

Arya listened to Maya's experience and offered a perspective that shifted her understanding. "Fundraising," she said, "is less about pitching and more about listening. It's a dialogue, not a monologue. Investors want more than just a good product; they want a founder who understands the market, listens to feedback, and adapts."

Maya reflected on what had happened. She was focused on her efforts to impress and missed the importance of understanding the investors' perspectives and concerns. Maya wanted them to hear what she had to say and forgot that she also needed to listen. She needed to ask them more questions and create interest in her business, not just execute her pitch flawlessly. The secret was the art of listening. And that was just the start of it.

More than encouraging Maya to harness her listening skills, Arya also shared possible alternatives to fund her startup and other important skills she needed to hone to raise capital. Maya realized she needed a concrete plan—an effective framework to build and secure her startup funds more confidently. She realized that there was more she needed to learn about raising capital. Now armed with these new insights, Maya became more excited and determined to pursue her fundraising efforts. Arya laid out the different steps and paths to raising money, and this started to make something click for Maya.

Like Maya, you may already have tried your own approach (and wonder why it isn't working), or you're just starting to look for ways to fund your startup but don't have a solid strategy yet.

Arya began to sketch out an iceberg on the back of a napkin. She explained to Maya that there is so much under the surface. The founder has done a lot of work behind the scenes to raise funds not stated in the press release.

Let's dig deeper into the Funding Framework and build the crucial fundraising and relationship-building skills to grow your startup. This is drawn from my experience and that of the founders I have worked with.

STORYTELLING

ORGANIZATION

OUTREACH

CLOSING

Your experiences may vary, and others' advice might diverge, but I've been lucky to draw on the insights of several investors. Follow Maya's journey in the pages ahead, use this book as a travel guide, and hop to the pages that are most relevant as you navigate the startup landscape in the future. Here, you will find the skills and strategies that differentiate successful fundraising efforts from telling your story to closing a "yes" with the right investors. Let's go!

Chapter 1

Introduction to Fundraising

The startup world is known for billions of dollars of investor money minting "unicorns" or young private companies valued at a billion dollars or more. This term, coined by Aileen Lee of Cowboy Ventures, has come to define the idea of success in Silicon Valley and across the world of startups and technology-enabled businesses everywhere.

Let's revisit Maya's first steps of her fundraising journey. Following the advice she received; Maya shifted her mindset to the fact that fundraising was not just about securing capital for her startup but also about building on several essential skills. Next was to plan, weigh, and choose the right funding options for her startup. She also recognized that she needed to consider other factors, such as investor relationships, communication, and long-term vision alignment in raising capital.

When it comes to the types of funding, startups, and conventional businesses differ significantly. If you're a startup founder with rapid growth and scalability in mind, you would likely need a substantial upfront investment. This is where equity funding, usually from venture capitalists, becomes essential. These investors are on the lookout for startups that promise exponential growth and massive returns.

On the other hand, if you're starting a conventional business with steady growth ambitions, some kind of credit or debt financing maybe more suitable. You can opt for loans or credit lines that are ideal for businesses with consistent cash flows and less aggressive growth plans (and cash needs). An infusion of capital from friends and family doesn't hurt either. "Bootstraping", or self-financing from free cashflow from your sales, is another route if you're aiming for gradual growth without much external investment. Let's sum up the types of funding you can consider:

Types of Funding

Equity Funding: Ideal for startups targeting rapid growth and large-scale market penetration. Equity investors, like venture capitalists, seek exponential growth and potentially large returns on their investments.

Debt Financing: More suitable for businesses with steady cash flows and less aggressive growth plans. This type of funding involves loans or credit lines. It is usually not the preferred route for startups due to the lack of immediate profitability and cash flow. Some founders get Venture Debt or asset-based financing to fund equipment, but this is often contingent on raising far more equity first from VCs.

Bootstrap Funding: Self-funding or using personal finances or revenues generated from customers. This method is common for small businesses that aim to grow organically without external funding.

Raising Equity May Not Be Right for You

One of the most important decisions you'll make as an entrepreneur is how to fund your startup. You need to understand the implications of that choice because it will be highly consequential for the future of your business.

I've navigated these waters during the early days of my first startup, weighing the pros and cons of equity vs. debt funding. The reality is that raising equity might not be the right choice for every startup. Weigh the advantages and disadvantages with an experienced advisor or mentor. Through my experiences and those of others in the startup ecosystem, I've learned that this decision hinges on several considerations:

1. **Nature of Your Business:** The type of business you're running plays a crucial role in deciding whether to raise equity. For instance, if you're engaged in a deep tech venture related to sectors like space, energy, or biotech, there might be grants available that are non-dilutive. This is ideal because it allows you to fund your research and development without giving up a stake in your company.

2. **Business Model:** If your business operates more like an agency or consultancy, where the revenue model is based on providing services, equity funding may not be suitable. In such cases, you're not selling a product but selling your expertise and time. Bootstrapping, where you reinvest the profits into the business, often makes more sense. Ultimately, maintaining full ownership and control over your business operations and direction is desirable.

3. **Growth Rate and Scale:** High-growth startups without consistent cash flow from operations that need significant capital upfront to scale rapidly might find equity funding more appropriate. If the capital required is for fixed assets, then bank financing or leasing is a lower-cost option. If the capital for high growth is used for building products, early customer acquisition, or intangible assets, then equity makes more sense. However, taking on debt might be more suitable for businesses with a moderate growth rate. Equity investors typically look for large returns, which only high-growth companies can feasibly promise. A credit line that finances accounts receivable from consistent recurring revenues may be an option later.

4. **Control and Ownership**: Equity funding often means giving up a portion of your company. If maintaining control and ownership is a priority, then debt financing or bootstrapping might be more appropriate. This is particularly relevant for founders who wish to retain decision-making authority and long-term vision without external pressures.

5. **Future Goals and Exit Strategies**: Your long-term goals and potential exit strategies also influence this decision. If you're looking to build a sustainable business without necessarily aiming for a large-scale exit like an IPO or acquisition, then bootstrapping or debt might be preferable. This is the path for the vast majority of businesses in the world. Equity makes more sense if you're aiming for aggressive growth with a future exit of some kind that would benefit both you and your equity investors.

Take time to carefully assess these factors to determine the most suitable funding option for your startup. Remember, the right choice will align with your business model, growth expectations, and vision for the company's future.

In the early days of Arya's first startup, she was making steady progress, growing modestly but consistently. Her product was initially well-received, and she had a growing base of loyal customers. However, the growth rate wasn't explosive—she was looking at no more than 10 percent increase month-to-month, which, while good in some ways, wasn't the hyper-growth typically sought by venture capitalists.

You may be faced with a very similar situation. Experiencing modest growth led Arya to a crucial realization: equity funding might not be the best path for her. The pressure to deliver exponential growth and the potential loss of control to equity investors didn't align with the vision. She was building a business that needed to prioritize more long-term viability over a rapid "Venture" scale. So, Arya explored alternative funding options that better suited that growth trajectory:

- **Bootstrapping**: Arya focused on generating revenue through her initial product and reinvesting profits back into the business. This approach allowed her to grow at a pace that made sense for her.

- **Working Capital Facilities**: As sales increased, she considered financing options based on her receivables. This approach provided her with the necessary funds to invest in scaling heroperations without diluting equity.

- **Grants and Non-Dilutive Funding:** For specific projects, especially those involving research and development, Arya investigated grants and other non-dilutive funding sources. This was particularly relevant when she was exploring new technologies that required great upfront investment but had the potential for significant long-term impact.

- **Friends and Family Funding**: Arya used this less formal route, which could provide her with more flexible terms and lower expectations regarding immediate returns.

Making these funding choices involved a thorough evaluation of her current financial health, future revenue projections, and overall business strategy. It was essential to balance the need for capital with the desire to maintain the integrity of Arya's vision and control over the company's direction. Her second startup was funded with more capital from corporate investment, and the growth path was faster.

Understanding these different funding types and aligning them with your startup's specific needs and goals is critical. Arya discovered that for her first startup, the best funding for a business is not a VC's term sheet but a customer's purchase order. *Your goal is not just to secure funds but to choose the right kind of funds* that can propel your business forward while also considering your core values and long-term objectives. In the next section, we'll tackle how you can evaluate these options and make the best decisions for your startup's unique journey.

Deciding Between Equity vs. Debt

Part of your decision-making process in choosing between equity and debt funding includes several considerations, including the following key factors: investor quality, cost of capital, dilution concerns, and market conditions. All these factors will directly impact your company's growth and your role as a startup entrepreneur.

Investor Reputation and Quality: When considering raising equity capital, the reputation and quality of the investor are paramount. Equity investors, particularly in startups, are not just funding sources but also partners who can offer mentorship, connections, and guidance. Their reputation can significantly impact your startup's prospects.

Cost of Capital and Cash Flow: For debt funding, a critical consideration is the cost of capital. This includes the interest rate and the pace at which the debt needs to be repaid. It's essential to assess whether your startup can feasibly manage these repayments based on its capacity to generate cash flow from operations.

Convertible Notes and SAFE (Simple Agreement for Future Equity): In the early stages, where the company's valuation is uncertain, instruments like convertible notes or SAFE can be used. **Convertible notes** are agreements where the investment initially may be a form of debt but converts into equity at a later stage, usually during a priced equity round. They are suitable when the company is still finding its product-market fit and is not ready for a Series A round. A SAFE is a special financial instrument startups often use to raise capital. Unlike traditional equity or debt instruments, a SAFE is not a loan and doesn't accrue interest. It's a contractual agreement between the startup and investors, providing the investors with the right to convert their investment into equity at a future date, usually at the occurrence of a specified event like the next funding round.

The key advantage of a SAFE is its simplicity and flexibility. It has become the most common way to raise money today, according to recent research from Peter Walker of Carta. It defers the need to determine the company's valuation immediately, which can be particularly challenging for early-stage startups. Instead, the conversion into equity typically occurs during a significant funding event, like a Series A round, based on a pre-agreed discount or valuation cap. Another crucial aspect of SAFEs is that they do not have a maturity date. This means that if the startup fails, SAFE holders do not have the same claim to the company's assets as debt holders might. These characteristics underscore the high-risk, high-reward nature of investing in startups.[1] Today, the SAFE is the standard. As Elizabeth Yin of Hustle Fund writes in *Raise Millions*, "Raising money through post-money SAFEs is often the easiest and most cost-effective way to fundraise for early startups."

Moreover, with SAFEs, there's no immediate need to amend a corporation's certificate of incorporation to authorize and establish the rights of the preferred stock that the SAFE may convert into. This can streamline the fundraising process, as the primary negotiation points often boil down to the investment amount and the valuation cap.[2]

---

[1] Dennis Craig, "What You Should Know About SAFEs," Cooley LLP, February 20, 2023, https://www.cooleygo.com/what-you-should-know-about-safes/#:~:text=A%20SAFE%20has%20no%20accruing,not%20have%20a%20maturity%20date

[2] Côme Laffay, "Raising with a SAFE," Open VC, December 18, 2023, https://www.openvc.app/blog/safe

Dilution Concerns: From a founder's perspective, dilution is a major concern. When you raise equity, you give away a portion of your company. It's crucial to ensure that the dilution is offset by the value the investment brings in terms of both capital and other resources. You need to be mindful of how much of the business you retain after dilution and whether this aligns with your long-term vision for the company. This has implications for control of the business and how much you will be left with as a shareholder.

Valuation and Future Fundraising: The valuation at which you raise money impacts future fundraising rounds significantly. Raising at a higher valuation may seem attractive as it leads to less dilution, but it sets higher expectations for future growth and subsequent rounds. This can be a double-edged sword, as it might create challenges in maintaining momentum and meeting inflated expectations.

Runway and Sustainability: Another factor to consider is how long the funds will last (runway) and how this aligns with your business plan. Raising more capital might seem like a safe bet, but it often comes with greater dilution. Balancing the amount of capital raised with the runway needed to achieve your next milestones is critical.

Market Conditions and Timing: External factors like market conditions and economic environments play a role. During certain periods, equity funding might be more accessible, while in others, debt or convertible instruments might be more feasible.

Now we've talked a little about the tools and materials, let's discuss the art of connecting and building relationships with investors.

Building Great Investor Relationships

Raising capital is more than presenting forecasts and business plans; it's about building and nurturing relationships with potential investors. Picture your investors as long-term business partners. If these investors choose to fund your startup, they will be part of your business journey for many years, so compatibility and mutual understanding are essential. Lean in. Listen carefully.

One of the first things to consider is compatibility with your investors. Their involvement level, whether they are hands-off or prefer to be deeply involved in your business, will significantly impact your working dynamics. More than the capital they bring to the table, the kind of relationship you foresee having with them is equally important. Remember that not all investors have the same approach. Some may prefer to give you the funds and step back, while others might want to be actively involved. Understanding their investment style and how they prefer to engage with their portfolio companies are important details you can observe. This information can often be gleaned through past interactions, blogs, podcasts, or speaking to their current or past portfolio company founders.

Effectively communicating your vision and understanding the investor's perspective is vital. Learn what they value in the spaces they invest in and how they perceive success. This will not only help you align your startup goals but also build a foundation for a transparent and productive relationship. A skill often overlooked is the ability to research and target the right investors. This involves understanding their investment thesis, the sectors they are interested in, and their typical investment stages. Utilizing platforms like LinkedIn, analyzing their blog posts or media interviews, and networking within the industry can provide valuable insights into their investment strategy and preferences.

You also need investors to understand why the perfect time to invest is now. Challenge them. As Marvin Liao of Diaspora Ventures describes, "It's a good thing if a founder challenges me respectively on my assumptions of the market and is able to educate me on the upcoming changes in the industry that were coming and how that would be unlocked for their business."

Fundraising often involves challenging negotiations and discussions. Don't burn bridges! The world is small, and you will run into people in other places. Maintaining a positive relationship is a skill that can determine the success of your fundraising efforts.

Whether you're discussing valuation, terms of investment, or future expectations, relationship-building when capital raising is a skill worth growing. Learn who your investors are, what they bring beyond the capital, and how you can work together towards a common goal. Mastering this skill will get you the right kind of support for your startup's journey.

Now, Maya's determined to take the next steps to find the right partners who align with her startup's ethos and future goals. Let's see what happens next.

Chapter 2

Storytelling and Messaging That Investors Expect

InsightAI is a product born from Maya's technical expertise and her passion for helping small businesses succeed. Her product could become a highly relevant and impactful offering in the market. The advanced analytics platform utilizes artificial intelligence, including machine learning, to aid small businesses with data integration, automated reporting, and predictive analytics in their daily operations.

Maya began reaching out to her network to find professional investors but soon realized how important her narrative would be. While she met with various angels and VCs, sharing her enthusiasm and showcasing the basic version of her product, she didn't have many customers, and there were no existing investors to validate or back her project yet. The venture capital firms Maya approached were looking for more advanced startups with proven market traction. After several tries, she began to think that maybe she was pitching to the wrong audience.

She remembered the room of VCs who were not interested enough in her business. More questions kept racing through her mind: How and where would she find the right investors? Who can lead her to the right people? How can she know which investor to approach? Who among them is interested in her specific startup? What was her story?

Prashanth's Story: The Right Investors at Every Stage

Maya's story was somehow similar to another founder's. Prashant, a determined Boston entrepreneur, had built an early version of his groundbreaking enterprise software solution. However, he faced a significant challenge: validating the existence of a market for his product. Eager to secure funding, Prashant reached out to his network, hoping to find professional investors who could help propel his venture forward.

Flying from Boston to Silicon Valley, he began visiting numerous VC firms and enthusiastically pitching his product. "I've built this," he would say, "I think it's really great." Despite his excitement, he faced a common startup dilemma—he had a basic, early version of the product with few customers and no existing investors. His efforts introduced his company to a group of well-known investors that provided capital to later-stage businesses, meaning they were too advanced for his current stage. This led to a series of rejections.

When I met and talked with Prashant, I had a few things in mind that I wanted to share concerning "market risk" that you can also apply. If the primary risk is related to distribution from large companies, like implementing software in Prashant's case, you can target experts connected in your space who are willing to make small angel investments. These could include CTOs, CIOs, or partners in big systems integration consulting firms. This move can be strategic. Such investors might recommend your product to their peers or companies, expanding your customer base and providing you with credibility. "Smart money" is not always a VC fund.

Emphasize finding investors who understand your market and stage of growth, ensuring they also align with your company's needs. Note that those investors with market knowledge offer some validation that your solution meets a genuine need. At the same time, the right investors can provide enough capital to allow you to accelerate product development or launching in the market. Recognize who can significantly contribute to your success based on your company's stage and relevance to their expertise. This is an important part of the investor outreach phase of the framework, as we will expand on later in Chapter 5.

Describing Your Business as a Product

Positioning your business as a product is crucial when seeking investment. Like any product, your business will attract different types of investors, each with unique motivations and expectations. Understanding different types of angel investors and venture capitalists and knowing how to tailor your pitch to meet their specific needs are vital aspects of successful fundraising. Identifying them can help you effectively communicate your business's potential, shape the trajectory of your startup, and potentially lead to more successful investor relationships in the future. However, approaching them too early can consume your precious time without generating some traction when, in fact, more customer and technical progress would be a better use of the time you spend in investor meetings. Building a great company worth investing in is the goal, not fundraising.

Types of Angel Investors

There are diverse types of angel investors, each with unique motivations and value propositions. Understanding these differences can help you target the right investors and tailor your pitch effectively.

- **High Net Worth Individuals:** High net-worth individuals often invest in startups driven by personal experiences, passions, or solving problems that have personally affected them. For example, an investor who has experienced healthcare challenges or encountered such issues in their own family might be keen on supporting startups that improve patient-at-home monitoring or a new brain scanning approach. This personal connection fuels their passion and commitment to the cause, making them likely to invest in companies that align with their personal experiences and values. One medical technology founder I know raised over $50 million from only angel investors because they were mission-aligned and did not have the aggressive growth expectations of some VCs.

- **Industry Experts:** These angels have significant experience in specific fields, such as clinicians or executives, who understand industry decision-making and buying behavior. While these expert investors do not run the company, they offer critical support such as valuable advice, customer introductions, potential hires, and access to other industry-relevant angels. Among the types of angels, those with industry expertise are particularly valuable for their network, knowledge, and potential to provide significant support to startups beyond just financial investment.

- **Angel Networks or Communities:** These groups consist of individuals who invest together, often pooling their capital to make larger investments. They can be generalists or have various specializations and operate in a more hands-off manner, such as those found on platforms like AngelList. However, they take time to rally their audience and often may only be able to take a small allocation compared to institutional investors like VCs.

Understanding these types of angel investors and their unique value propositions is essential for tailoring your pitch and securing the right support for your startup. By targeting the right investors and leveraging their strengths, you can significantly enhance your startup's chances of success.

Differences Between Angels and Venture Capitalists (VC)

Looking into different investors, you should also note that angel investors and venture capitalists have different expectations and time horizons.

Return Expectations: Angels typically look at individual deals with the hope of doubling or tripling their investment, while VCs manage pooled capital with a high failure rate and seek investments that can potentially return their entire fund. As Elizabeth Yin, general partner of Hustle Fund, says, "VCs look for startups that can give them a 100x return while angel investors have different, often lower, expectations. If you raise money from VCs, make sure the market can be measured in billions of dollars. Consider raising funds from angel investors if your market is smaller, and have conversations about what success looks like for them."

Venture capitalists expect high returns to offset portfolio losses, aiming for investments that can yield double-digit returns and potentially return the entire fund. This means they look for startups with the potential to reach substantial valuations and often achieve far greater than twenty times returns.

In the history of VC fund returns and my own experience, some companies have returned multiples of hundreds or even thousands of times the initial investment. But for every one of these, there are a hundred portfolio companies that do not generate this outcome, and a large number of venture funds never return their cost of capital, making the job of generating good returns exceptionally difficult for venture capital fund managers[3].

---

[3] Institutional Investor "Big VC Funds Are Underperforming Smaller Ones and Their Future Is Dim" https://www.institutionalinvestor.com/article/2cjotgawx 7nn70st06k8w/portfolio/big-vc-funds-are-underperforming-smaller-ones-and-their-future-is-dim

Perspective on Investment: Venture capitalists need to see the potential for a startup to achieve significant scale, such as reaching hundreds of millions in sales and becoming worth billions, to consider it "venture-scale." As Dave Anderson, founding partner of Beat Ventures, explains, "I've noticed that many founders struggle when asked about the long-term vision of their company. This question often arises: "Where do you see this company in seven to ten years?" or "What's an ideal exit strategy?" The best founders use this opportunity to articulate a clear, compelling vision for the future of their company and the broader impact they aim to achieve. They share not only their strategic plans but also their passion, painting a vivid picture of the meaningful difference they intend to make in the world."

Creating Different Conversations: When pitching to angel investors, focus on forward-looking growth and immediate milestones. When pitching to VCs, emphasize the long-term potential and scalability of the business to justify the high return expectations.

Long-Term Commitment: Venture capital funds are typically illiquid for several years, which means VCs have a long-term commitment and seek substantial returns from their investments to distribute to their limited partners.

Pitching for Angel Investors and Venture Capitalists

When preparing to pitch your startup to investors, whether they are angel investors or venture capitalists (VCs), it's essential to understand their distinct priorities and what captures their interest.

Angel Investors: Team and Vision

Angel investors are often drawn to the team behind the startup and the compelling vision they present. They want to believe in the team and the dream. This means they are looking for a talented group with relevant experience and a deep understanding of the market they're entering.

For example, if you're pitching to angels for a startup focused on AI-powered student tutoring, they would be excited by a team that includes members with prior success in the education or gaming industries.

In fact, Sundeep Ahuja, who founded Climate Capital, which began as one of the first angel syndicates to invest in climate tech, says, "First-time founders building in a large, complex market without any industry veterans advising or on the team is a red flag." They would appreciate the vision of improving student outcomes through personalized coaching and leveraging innovative technology like AI. Personal connections and shared frustrations can also play a significant role in gaining angel investors' interest, as they often invest in ideas they can personally relate to or already believe in passionately.

Venture Capitalists: Metrics and Traction

On the other hand, venture capitalists place greater emphasis on quantifiable metrics and evidence of momentum. VCs want to believe in the metrics and the momentum. They will focus more on your Key Performance Indicators (KPIs), growth rates, and overall progress since the last funding round. VCs are also more interested in seeing consistent growth in metrics like user acquisition, revenue, or market penetration. You need to know this inside out.

Shawn Xu, partner of Lowercarbon Capital, finds this to be a bigger problem than you might think. "I wish more founders knew their unit economics 'cold.' Above and beyond is knowing the unit economics of their competitors by heart and understanding how they're benchmarked over time. One founder knew exactly how their economics would evolve over time, down to specific milestones by month. That founder might be off, but the fact that they thought through the assumptions was impressive. You'd be surprised how many founders can't speak to this."

Since they invest in trends and progress over time, they aim to support startups demonstrating scalability and market leadership potential. Moreover, VCs operate within specific investment theses, focusing on particular stages, sectors, or business models where they have expertise and believe they can add significant value. They have also promised their Limited Partners (LPs) who have invested in them to invest based on this thesis.

To pitch to angels and VCs effectively, tailor your presentation to high-light what matters most to each group. For angel investors, emphasize the strength of your team, their relevant experience, and the compel-ling vision driving your startup. If you're targeting VCs, showcase your measurable progress, growth metrics, and how your startup fits within their investment thesis and broader market trends. Team, Traction, and Total Addressable Market matter to everyone, but they usually weigh differently. As mentioned in Chapter 1, get to know your investors and understand what drew them to past investments and what risk they are willing to take on.

Different Stages of Fundraising

Aside from identifying the types of investors to target, understanding the various fundraising stages is also crucial for strategically positioning your startup in the eyes of potential investors. Each stage represents a different phase of growth and development, accompanied by distinct investor expectations and metrics.

Pre-seed and Seed Stage

At the pre-seed and seed stages, your primary focus is building your product or service and acquiring initial customers. As Martin Tobias of Incisive Ventures describes, "Pre-seed is post-angel or accelerator round with the expectation of $200,000 to $300,000 already raised from friends and family to create an MVP." Investors of all kinds at this stage are particularly interested in the strength of your team and the potential of your market.

You can further assess by asking yourself these questions: Are you at the stage where you've built a product and sold it? How big is your team? How much traction have you developed with customers? This early phase often requires leveraging warm introductions and positive word of mouth to capture investor attention. This may need additional clarification depending on whether it is hardware or software. As you proceed, stay curious and learn as much as you can.

Series A

Moving into the Series A stage, the emphasis shifts to demonstrating product-market fit. Investors expect growing revenue, an expanding user base, and solid metrics validating your business model. Metrics and traction become more critical at this point. In addition, this is where startups need to prove their ability to scale and sustain growth. Investors may ask a lot of you at this stage because any financial projections you have should be rock solid.

And yet, as Jonathan Charles of Samsung Catalyst Fund says, "I often find that Founders don't fully have their financial models 'down cold' to the point that they can discuss in a fair amount of detail (e.g., various revenue drivers and details on expenses) without prep-time or referring to some 'finance' person. The Founder can help an investor assess not only the business model overall but also the Founder's understanding of how things can change over time and what impact this will have on sales." He adds that, "It's not about the final numbers. Rather, it's about how a Founder got to those numbers, how intellectually honest he is on what causes change to the business, and how such change illicit responses in terms of team ability/performance and flexibility/resiliency of the business model."

Series B and Beyond

For startups entering Series B and beyond, the focus shifts towards scalability, significant revenue growth, and establishing market leadership—three things that founders need to highlight at this point. Investors at this stage are looking for companies with proven business models poised for substantial expansion. Startups seeking Series B funding and beyond must demonstrate a clear path to achieving market dominance and delivering substantial returns to investors.

Each fundraising stage demands a tailored narrative and set of metrics that align with investor expectations. As your startup progresses through these stages, your pitch should evolve to reflect the milestones achieved and the growth trajectory ahead. Understanding where your startup fits within this spectrum—from early development to scaling operations—is essential for effectively targeting the right investors and securing funding.

Samantha Huang, principal of BMW iVentures, says, "Closing a round in today's challenging environment requires founders to make sure that their companies meet the comparable business metrics and milestones of similar venture-backed companies in their cohort. A Series B SaaS company, for example, needs to make sure it hits the revenue and growth metrics of what venture capitalists generally expect to see for Series B SaaS companies. For the most part, you can't be selling on the vision of some cool product anymore."

Raul: Seizing Opportunity with Strategic Fundraising

Raul, founder and CEO of a thriving software startup, found himself at a crucial juncture in early 2020. With his company poised to scale and expand its market presence, he knew that securing the right funding at the right time would be pivotal for its growth trajectory.

As the pandemic loomed, Raul strategically planned to raise a Series B round just before its onset. This timing proved fortuitous as it allowed his company to accumulate a substantial cash reserve, providing a crucial buffer against the uncertainties brought by the pandemic.

However, the story didn't end there. As Raul navigated through the Series B funding process, he caught the attention of several late-stage crossover funds—entities known for their aggressive investment strategies in transitioning from hedge funds to venture capital. Despite the interest, he maintained a strategic stance of non-availability, subtly signaling that his focus was on scaling rather than immediate fundraising.

This deliberate approach created a sense of scarcity and heightened interest among potential investors. When the time was ripe, Raul swiftly moved to capitalize on the heightened investor enthusiasm. With a pipeline of interested parties, negotiations for the Series B round proceeded efficiently, culminating in a successful raise from one of the most aggressive crossover funds of 2021.

The funding round was not just about securing capital but also validating his vision and the company's potential in the eyes of sophisticated investors. The high valuation attached to the raise reflected confidence in the startup's market position and growth prospects.

Now armed with a significant cash infusion, Raul's company has a comfortable runway ahead. This financial flexibility allows him to focus on executing strategic initiatives, scaling operations, and achieving milestones to further solidify the company's market leadership. Profitability, if he chooses, is also within his reach.

How Much to Raise

Determining the right amount to raise in a fundraising round influences a startup's growth trajectory and future financial health. It may seem like grabbing as much capital as you can when you can is always the right approach, but that depends on a few variables. Here are key factors you should consider and evaluate to arrive at better decisions on the amount you're raising for your startup:

Strategic Business Goals

Instead of approaching fundraising as simply a means to gain funds and extend the runway, learning to align your fundraising amount with your business objectives is the right move. Investors expect more than hearing about the financial needs of your startup. It would be wiser to emphasize the next step of your business, like rolling out a product or reaching specific industries or categories in the market. This strategic approach involves identifying specific milestones such as product development, market expansion, or scaling operations requiring additional capital. Elizabeth Yin of Hustle Fund in *Raise Millions* states that the best time to fundraise is "Just after you have hit one of these milestones, meaning that the business has now progressed to a new point than in the past."

Investment in Growth

As an entrepreneur, you can articulate how the capital raised will drive growth and enhance your startup's capabilities. Whether for hiring key talent, investing in sales and marketing efforts, or scaling infrastructure, the fundraising amount should directly support achieving significant business milestones.

Stress details of how your business will require you to raise a certain amount, but this unlocks the next stage of growth—the way that completing a level of a video game unlocks the next stage of opportunity. This clarity helps investors understand the purpose of the funds and the potential return on their investment.

Finding Compatible Investors

Vision for Future Business

Investors are interested in supporting startups that have a clear vision for future success. Aim to communicate not just your current needs but also your aspirations for the business. As Marvin Liao of Diaspora Ventures describes it, "Make sure it's really clear why you are the outlier and share what you think is happening in your sector and why it still matters, i.e., what are the confluence of trends that show something is changing in the market."

Have a clear picture of what you want your business to be and what the things you need to do. This forward-thinking approach demonstrates ambition and strategic foresight, which aligns investor expectations with your startup's long-term objectives. Make it clear that you intend to get there essentially with or without them. The future is bright, and your intention is clear, so you can express politely but confidently how you would love to have them join you on this journey and that you will do everything possible to succeed.

The advantage of doing this can be huge, as Jonathan Charles of Samsung Catalyst Fund maintains, "The CEO has to be able to sell the team, product, and vision to the right kinds of potential investors. I've literally seen a growing performance gap between charismatic CEOs with sales skills with a network vs. the more introverted CEOs with no network, even if both are technical and operating in the deep tech investment market."

Avoiding Status Quo Thinking

Fundraising should not be solely about maintaining the status quo. A vital fundraising skill you can learn is to articulate how additional capital will enable the company to innovate, grow market share, and achieve a competitive advantage. That's why it's crucial to reframe your discussion from immediate financial needs to strategic investment for future growth. It's best to ensure investors see the potential for substantial returns and value creation, not just covering today's cash burn rate.

Researching Your Investors

Now that you have an idea of what investor category suits your fundraising stage and business type, it's time to conduct thorough research on potential investors. But hold your horses because this isn't about making the typical list of leading VC firms, and you're done. To build a successful fundraising strategy, you need to understand individual investors. Researching will also entail a great amount of time and effort. But believe me, doing this assignment will be worth it.

Focusing on the Individual, Not Just the Firm

It's common for entrepreneurs to compile lists of top investment firms based on reputation or prominence. However, my advice is not solely to focus on the firm's name recognition. Instead, research on the individual partner who could potentially lead your investment round. Factors such as their social media presence, past investments, and professional background can offer valuable insights into their investment philosophy and compatibility with your startup's goals.

Building Long-Term Relationships

Beyond the initial funding round, it's also important to consider the long-term implications of the investor relationship. Founders should look for investors who share a future vision compatible with their business goals. Selecting an investor who not only provides capital but also acts as an advocate and champion for your company within their firm is a gold mine. They won't be there just for the "now"; they are the kind of investors who can push you to grow and improve your business. This advocate should be a general partner who can play a pivotal role in influencing investment decisions and can significantly impact your startup's trajectory.

Maximizing All Points of Contact

Building connections with individuals within the investor's network is also essential throughout the engagement process. Associates, business development professionals, and support staff often serve as gatekeepers to key decision-makers. Building positive relationships with these stakeholders can enhance your credibility and facilitate access to influential figures within the firm.

Approaching the Right Person

Effective communication with investors involves approaching the right person within the organization. While initial contact may be made through associates or support staff, the goal eventually is to engage directly with a general partner. These senior figures hold decision-making authority and can facilitate the necessary resources and support for your startup's growth.

Successful Partnerships Thrive

Marvin Liao of Diaspora Ventures, previously head of the 500 Startups Accelerator, emphasizes that he wishes founders would ask "Why they [founders] should take our money and how we can help them in their business."

Understanding the importance of strategic alignment between startups and investors can be the key to a successful fundraising journey. Ask them to share some examples of startups that successfully aligned with an investor's thesis and resulted in mutually beneficial partnerships. Additionally, we'll also explore how identifying investors that support your future ambitions can lead to long-term success.

Strategic Alignment with Corporate Venture Capital Firms

Corporate venture capital (CVC) firms often provide more than just funding; they offer strategic benefits such as distribution channels and industry expertise. Startups that align with the strategic goals of CVCs can leverage these advantages for substantial growth.

A startup developing advanced medical imaging software raised funds from a leading medical device company's venture arm. This strategic alignment allow the startup to secure funding and integrate its software with the medical devices produced by the investor, thereby enhancing product functionality and gaining access to a broader market through the investor's established distribution networks.

Similarly, a financial technology startup focused on small business payment solutions partnered with a mature financial services corporation. This relationship provided the startup with the capital needed for development and gave it access to the corporation's extensive customer base, facilitating rapid scaling of its product offerings.

Other investors may leverage their corporate networks or corporate investor base like Jay Eum, founding managing partner of GFT Ventures, who explains, "Leveraging our corporate connections and understanding their roadmaps, product technology roadmaps, what gaps they're trying to fill, what sort of level of urgency and priorities they have is something that we bring from our corporate backgrounds."

Partnering with Investors Support Portfolio Companies

When startups partner with investors who share their vision and future ambitions, thecollaboration often results in long-term success. Such investors provide not only capital but also mentorship, industry insights, and valuable connections. Sundeep Ahuja, managing partner of Climate Capital, says more founders need to ask his firm, "What can you do for us about which we might not know? What are all the resources your firm has that I can take advantage of?"

Many institutional venture firms incubate founders or have accelerator programs that help with downstream fundraising after demo day. Separately, funds like Uncork Ventures have a talent-oriented platform team to support founders. Sierra Ventures helps with content and insights to help founders with marketing.

An example of a visible successful company that partnered with investors to share their vision and ambitions is Airbnb. This company received early investment and mentorship from Y Combinator. This leading accelerator program not only provided capital but also essential guidance. This support helped Airbnb pivot its business model and scale effectively from humble beginnings.

Government and Institutional Investors

Government and institutional investors often aim to foster economic development and technological innovation in specific regions. Startups that align with these goals can benefit from significant support, including funding, infrastructure, and access to local markets.

A Gulf state government invested in a technology startup with the condition that the startup would establish a development center within the state, which was amenable to all parties. This investment gave the startup the necessary capital and facilitated its expansion into new markets, creating jobs and contributing to the local economy.

The Investors' Full Support

Entrepreneurs should look for investors who share their vision and values. Compatibility in future ambitions ensures that the investor genuinely supports the startup's long-term goals.

For example, Peter Fenton of Benchmark is renowned for his role as an exceptional board member. Startups that have partnered with him have benefited from his strategic insights, mentorship, and network, contributing to their sustained growth and success.

Similarly, firms like Andreessen Horowitz provide extensive support to their portfolio companies, helping them navigate challenges and scale effectively, including talent (hiring), business development, and finding a future exit. Such investors, who go beyond mere capital provision, play a critical role in the success of the startups they back.

Finding Compatible Investors

Maya found her way out of her investor-hunting dilemma. At the pre-seed stage of her startup, she called Arya and got excellent fundraising advice. Start small. Maya joined a top accelerator program and trimmed down her list of angel investors who had industry expertise and connections. She was thorough in her research, making sure their backgrounds, philosophies, and goals matched her startup. She now knows the type of investors she will target and approach.

She was confident that their endorsement would serve as a powerful signal to market InsightAI, showcasing this analytics tool was a solution that met a real need. As she looked forward, she was foreseeing these investors recommending her product to their peers and companies. Now, it was time to prepare her content and organize the process for her fundraising strategy.

Chapter 3

Adopting a Strategic Fundraising Process

Maya had bumped into Ben, a former co-worker who also happened to be a startup founder. Ben was building a new e-commerce marketplace and had a captivating vision. Maya also shared about her startup, InsightAI, and how she flopped her first investor presentation.

"That was quite a learning experience. But I joined an accelerator program, so now I'm researching investors to add to my list. Then, I'll prepare for my next presentations."

"Well, that's good for you, Maya," Ben replied. "I've had several pitches already over the past weeks. Pretty neat, huh?"

"Wow, so what's your strategy? Can you let me in on your process, or maybe you can share some steps for your fundraising?" Maya's eyes were beaming as she waited for Ben to describe the "secret sauce" to his process.

Ben chuckled with a surprising revelation: "I really don't have any. These investors are all so different, and I'm just going to do my thing, y'know?"

Maya was surprised and stunned by what she heard and what Ben told her next.

Her friend didn't have a clear start and end date for raising funds. In his mind, he was just going to raise a million dollars. How Ben prepared for his presentation was even more startling. He would go to the whiteboard, start drawing things, and then tell investors how the world works and what he wants to do. Ben was trying to gather as many "yeses" as possible. But in reality, it was a great many "maybes." More than that, his presentation threw in an array of technical terms and industry jargon that often left investors clueless and later uninterested.

And here's another part of his epic strategy: rather than present the business, he wanted them to use the product right away. Once hooked, he thought, they would get excited to invest. The greatest blow to his process was deciding to switch his story too many times. When he heard a new thing or two from investors, he quickly jumped into that idea and changed his pitch.

Ben and the Demo

Let's see what we can learn from Ben's "everything-goes" strategy. Sales coach and author Zig Ziglar said, "If you aim at nothing, you'll hit it every time." And Ben sure hit that target all the time. Though this founder was set with an attractive vision and innovative product for his e-commerce startup, he didn't have an effective fundraising process, let alone a timeline.

First, Ben could've focused on sharing who he was and what he knew —offering a solution to an enormous problem. What he thought would be a good opportunity to show the founders who he was and the progress the company was making turned out to be a lost opportunity to make a good impression.

And his futuristic presentation? It turns out that investors can only invest in the business that the founder has today or one that can be very easily understood, in contrast to one that would take them a mental leap or two to be able to visualize things. You see, VCs are very smart people, but you need to talk to them like you were speaking to a smart high schooler. They are obviously capable of adult conversations but don't necessarily have all the exact market insights and technical knowledge you have. They don't know everything. How can they? So, simplicity is key. Not to mention, they have short attention spans, and many of them infamously enjoy social media too much!

Another thing that Ben could've considered is that investors will try to use the product but are more likely to do so after they have been bought into the team, have a total addressable market, and have a go-to-market strategy. Remember, a product without a clear business model does not make a startup.

This business model issue can be especially true in certain categories like hardware. Ian Campbell at Climate Capital points out, "Founders are seldom able to address essential questions like go-to-market strategy." He adds, "For hardware that has to be sold into a larger system—what is the sales cycle like, and how are you building a killer sales function internally to support it?"

Lack of customer discovery and research is frequently a sin of founders in the deep tech space. As Jonathan Charles, investment director of Samsung Catalyst Fund, explains: "A big red flag is having a 'build it and they will come' strategy vs. having a truly thoughtful customer discovery process and product-market fit game plan. Just having high-level value prop numbers (e.g., We have X percent higher performance and Y percent lower cost), which is not backed up by any customer discovery, is often not good enough for that new customer to buy. There is much more that goes into the buying decision. Founders need to tell investors about all the details that come from the customer alone, which should be translated into a coherent strategy."

Lastly, constantly changing the vision and trying something new out in every meeting lose investors in the conversation, and eventually, they lose interest. Often, you don't need to have too much technical explanation or jargon to drive your point. What they want to see is how you get from A to Z, coupled with a logical and intuitive story that they can follow.

You also don't need to be pitching the hottest new thing. Samantha Huang of BMW iVentures suggests, "As long as the fundamentals of your business work out, it doesn't matter if you're in a white-hot sector or not. Sometimes, the most unsexy industries make for the best businesses because no one else is looking at them and competing there. If you have the expertise and know-how in that area, you're in a better position starting a business there than in an area that's overhyped and overcrowded."

Similarly, Sundeep Ahuja of Climate Capital says, "Focus on sales and non-dilutive funding if investors are cool on your technology, focus on getting cash in the door another way so you have a strong business when the wheel comes back around. Build and be patient. A 'hot sector' could just be hot air, and there's no use trying to time the hype cycles. Go to market with the strongest, clearest value proposition possible and make your team appear undeniably ideal to tackle the challenge."

For founders, haphazard processes will never work, especially these days. The bar is high. Sorry, but your magician's hat and mystical wand won't do the trick. That's why it's crucial to have a process these days. Investor Marvin Liao of Diaspora Ventures reminds startup founders to just run a disciplined process and refuse the urge to be superficial. He emphasizes, "You need to run a tighter process than normal and do twice the outreach and conversations. Due diligence is also far more detailed, thorough, and longer than ever before."

Run a Strategic Process in Five Steps

Successfully raising funds requires a strategic and well-structured approach. This section provides a roadmap to help you build your fundraising process effectively so you can gain the necessary capital to fuel your startup.

1. Develop a Comprehensive Timeline

Creating a clear and realistic timeline is crucial. A ten to twelve-week timeline is typically aggressive yet feasible. This period should include the following key activities:

- **Research:** Spend the initial weeks researching potential investors who align with your startup's vision and industry.

- **Introductions and Meetings:** Aim to get introduced to investors and schedule meetings *within the first two to four weeks*. As Elizabeth Yin of Hustle Fund writes, "Follow up right after the call reiterating what you both talked about and send over any promised assets."

- **Demonstrating Momentum:** During these meetings, showcase your progress and the interest you've garnered from other potential investors.

This approach stems from my experience observing multiple cohorts while creating and leading the portfolio value team at 500 Startups and working closely with its Flagship Accelerator. It also incorporates insights and advice from several generations of leaders at that accelerator and other startup programs.

2. Secure a Lead Investor

A lead investor is pivotal in your fundraising journey. The lead should emerge by the midway point of your process. This timeline allows you to:

- **Assess Term Sheets:** Evaluate the term sheet presented by the lead investor carefully.

- **Do Your Due Diligence:** Have the diligence to ensure the terms align with your expectations and goals.

Having a lead investor also simplifies attracting other investors who can contribute to a third or half of the round, making the process more streamlined.

3. Understand Investor Expectations

We mentioned earlier that different investors have varying expectations and time horizons. Therefore, it's important to understand these to tailor your pitch appropriately:

- **Pre-Seed to Seed:** When raising pre-seed capital, meet with one or two seed funds to understand what traction metrics they require for seed-stage investments. This prepares you to meet the necessary milestones for future funding rounds.

- **Seed to Series A:** Similarly, when raising seed capital, engage with Series A investors to learn what KPIs (key performance indicators) they expect to see for their investment stage.

Martin Tobias of Incisive Ventures emphasizes the importance of these informational conversations to set clear targets for future rounds. "When raising pre-seed capital, take a few meetings with Seed funds. They won't invest but ask them what traction metrics they have to reach those Seed KPIs (The same might apply if raising a seed wherein you should talk to Series A investors). The key is to know where you are going."

4. Budgeting and Financial Planning

Proper financial planning is also critical so you can avoid running out of capital prematurely:

- **Overestimate Budgets:** Always plan for contingencies. It's advisable to add 25 percent to your budget to cover unforeseen expenses. This ensures you have enough runway to reach key milestones without returning for unexpected additional funding.

- **Plan for Long-term Goals:** You must also ensure your pre-seed or seed capital is sufficient to reach the next significant milestone, typically the KPIs required for the subsequent funding round.

5. Personalize Your Outreach

Effective communication with potential investors is vital whether it's through emails or personally. Stephen Nasser of OpenVC advises that cold emails should be highly personalized to avoid sounding generic. Personalized outreach can significantly increase the chances of securing a meeting and making a positive impression on potential investors.

Following these strategic principles, you can streamline your fundraising process, attract the right investors, and secure the capital needed to drive your startup's success.

Explanation of a Lead Investor

A lead investor plays a crucial role in fundraising, especially during a priced round. This investor not only provides a significant portion of the capital, as described earlier but also sets the terms of the investment, so there's a structure and transparent framework for other investors to follow. The importance of a lead investor stems from several key aspects.

First, a lead investor offers validation and confidence to other potential investors. Often, interested parties may express a willingness to invest but prefer to see a lead investor committed before they follow suit. This is because a lead investor's involvement signals a level of due diligence and confidence in the startup's potential, which can alleviate concerns among other investors who might be hesitant to be the first to commit. Yes, in most financial markets, investor behavior is herd-like. Essentially, a lead investor's commitment serves as an endorsement encouraging more investors to join the round.

In times when fundraising is more challenging (like at the time of writing), the need for a lead investor becomes even more apparent. Many venture capitalists may give soft no's, indicating they are not ready to invest unless someone else leads. This scenario highlights the psychological aspect of investment decisions, where fear of missing out (FOMO) can be a significant motivator. Potential investors often don't want to miss an opportunity others have deemed worthy. Seeing a lead investor involved can trigger this FOMO, which leads them to participate.

However, it is important to note that having a lead investor is not an absolute requirement to have a term sheet. Sometimes, startups might create their own term sheet or use a SAFE, presenting it to potential investors. Yet, the feedback "come back when you have a lead" usually implies that these investors are not ready to be the sole or first capital in. They want reassurance from someone else's due diligence and commitment, reflecting their cautious approach and the desire not to take the initial risk. This may be hard to hear when your heart and soul are invested in your business.

Based on my experience with many founders, I've seen that a successful approach involves having a lead investor who provides the term sheet. Because they are investing one-third to half, or sometimes more, of the round, they can set the terms. Some lead investors will condition their investments based on others who are also investing. However, once they lead the round, they should help close it by contacting other investors who might want to participate if they are not taking up the full round.

Some so-called "Party Rounds" can result in many investors who are not deeply committed, or worse, they quickly forget about you because their small investment didn't matter much to them. However, a great lead investor is careful and thoughtful about whom to share deal flow with and understands that founders want to join up with new investors who are well-aligned with their goals. It's important to remember that terms are nearly always nonbinding. Deals can fall through at the last minute for unforeseen reasons. Therefore, the reputation of the lead investor for following through is crucial for ensuring that you will ultimately have the money in the bank.

Avoid Using Fundraising Matchmakers or Brokers

While brokers and matchmakers promise to facilitate connections with investors, relying on them can often backfire, especially for early-stage ventures. And here's why:

- **Warm Intros vs. Cold Emails:** The best startups secure funding through warm introductions, not cold emails sent by brokers. Relying on brokers often signals to VCs that you lack the ability to navigate the fundraising landscape effectively. The best warm introductions come from current portfolio company founders or investors they trust.

- **Building Trust:** Directly connecting with investors yourself is crucial. It demonstrates your ability to find and earn the trust of those investors, a key component in successful fundraising.

- **Cost of Matchmakers:** Matchmakers and brokers can be expensive, often charging high fees for their services. This cost can be prohibitive, especially for early-stage startups with limited resources.

- **Limited Applicability:** While there may be some benefit to using investment banks for private placements at later stages to reach certain institutional investors, these circumstances do not apply to early-stage fundraising.

- **Success Fees Misconception:** Brokers might claim to guarantee substantial investments for a percentage fee. However, unlike investment banks that underwrite their offerings in IPOs, most brokers simply send emails without taking on any significant risk themselves.

- **Perception of Spam:** Emails from brokers or matchmakers are often perceived as spam by investors. An introduction from someone paid to send emails lacks the warm, trusted relationship necessary for a compelling pitch.

- **Time Constraints of Investors:** Investors are typically inundated with deal flow, making it unlikely that they will respond to pitches from unknown third parties. They prioritize deals forwarded by trusted contacts, reducing the effectiveness of cold emails from brokers.

Not all matchmakers and brokers are bad. Some good ones prefer to work with existing portfolio companies, only work off a success fee, and/or help you with your financial model or pitch deck. Some I know are, in fact, trusted by certain investors.

A bad sign is that they will work with any and everyone regardless of readiness when they should be vetting the best opportunities to bring to their network.

Do you think that an investment banker is necessary at later stages? Not so fast. In fact, according to Stephanie Rieben-de Roquefeuil, CEO of Diadem Capital and a New York-based fundraising expert, "Most Series C onwards start working with expensive investment bankers, which I find counterintuitive. Pre-seed through Series B. You don't have the network yet, but by the time you're a Series C, you should have talked to most VCs and growth shops."

Personal Investor Experiences

When seeking investment, I always emphasize the importance of finding investors who already believe in the future you're building. This was reinforced during a conversation with one successful angel investor and climate tech founder in San Francisco. He pointed out that it's crucial to align with investors who are naturally inclined toward your vision. He's raised repeated rounds of funding this way.

I focus on identifying individuals who share my chosen areas of interest. If I become interested in what they are building, I continue to engage and offer more value. Establishing relationships with investors whose investment thesis and expectations align with your vision is crucial. This approach makes it easier to gain their trust and support. It's about finding a natural compatibility with their existing beliefs and goals.

For example, my individual investment strategy as an angel investor involves finding intersections between different sectors, such as fintech, SaaS, and climate tech. I draw on my personal background and experiences to navigate these areas effectively. Rather than specializing narrowly, I identify synergies between various sectors, leveraging my broad expertise in making investment decisions. This allows me to bring unique insights and value to the companies I support. Many otherinvestors focus narrowly on areas like material science, AI, biotech, or new markets such as those using cryptocurrency and blockchain technology. Understanding when to bring in specialized knowledge is key to making successful investments.

Also, having been an expert instructor on Maven and for different VC firms, teaching B2B sales strategy for startup founders, I would emphasize these critical principles for success. As I've pointed out before, fundraising is very similar to sales. Here's my approach:

- **Get the Right Strategic Footing:** It's crucial to be strategic when it comes to market size and sectors. I teach founders to select the ideal industries based on a few criteria, meet decision-makers who need their products, and understand how these prospects think. The fundraising version of this targets people with a strong thesis fit.

- **Solve Valuable Problems for Your Future Customers:** Conducting world-class customer development is essential. Every company has big problems; identifying them is the secret to great customer development. This move, in turn, makes your product better and creates new channels for your business. Show investors your deep knowledge of customer pain points in the market you are focusing on.

- **De-risk Your Solutions for Decision Makers:** I emphasize the importance of building a pilot program to de-risk your startup's product or service for decision-makers. This makes it easier for them to advocate for you. Keep showing this traction to investors.

- **Develop Results That Produce Momentum:** Social proof is crucial. I teach founders to turn their first win into a compelling case study for others to follow. This builds momentum and credibility. Show that other VCs and respected angels are invested or already committed to the round.

While many Bens and Mayas are raising their startup capital, I hope there will be more investors who believe in them and support these founders in their portfolios.

I've always believed in empowering entrepreneurs to create positive change. It greatly influences my investment decisions and the companies I choose to support. This hands-on approach ensures that the entrepreneurs I work with receive the support they need to succeed. By sharing these experiences and insights, I hope to provide a clear understanding of how to navigate the complex world of investment and entrepreneurship so founders like Ben and Maya can have successful and impactful ventures.

Again, this is my personal experience as an investor and coach. Make sure that you ask questions of your individual venture firms. To understand where and how they can support you and change the odds for your startup.

Chapter 4

The Secret of a Great Pitch is Great Organization

The great Chinese military strategist Sun Tzu said, "Every great battle is won before it is ever fought." For founders, every funding is made possible before the pitch because you are prepared and organized.

Maya was sure she didn't want to end up like Ben. After several meet-ups with Arya, she got some fundraising pointers on how to have a solid, strategic, and adaptable process to follow. She set her timeline, did investor research aiming to find potential lead investors, and finalized her budget plans.

"Now let's get to the nitty-gritty part," Arya said, "making your pitch and presenting your startup to those investors."

Maya was a sponge, ready to soak up all the learnings she would receive from Arya that day. Then a question suddenly popped into her mind, "But Arya, I just have one question. Is it possible that investors could also be the ones to, you know, reach out to me instead?"

"Of course, absolutely!" Arya answered. "Remember what I said before about creating a FOMO? It's one of the proven strategies you can work with."

And I couldn't agree more with Arya. Remember Raul (not his real name), who told me how VCs would find out about him and his startup? His company was growing at that time, but the first thing that he'd always say was that he wasn't raising funds. When these VCs persisted, he'd fend them off and tell them now is not a good time.

Sounds contradictory? Many associates, particularly junior investment staff, reached out to him, but he would reply that he'd be happy to talk to them with one of the partners from their firm. Here's the good part: When the time came that he did want to raise, he created a lot of FOMO and pressure on top-tier VCs to invest in his round. This meant prioritizing speed. With this approach, he prioritized speed and ultimately raised a series B round from a top-tier investor. The best result was that he had no further need to raise capital in the future and reached profitability in 2023.

It's also possible for you to have Raul's experience in your fundraising journey. However, one leading factor in getting them to listen is how you pitch your startup and make a good presentation. This chapter focuses on the fundamental details of the organization phase of the framework—from preparing your pitch and presentation to creating your data room so you can hit those yeses effectively.

Developing Your Pitch

Maya wanted to share her pitch but was concerned about sending over too much information. How could she share enough information to get the meeting but not reveal some information or details that she would prefer to cover in person?

You can start developing a pitch by creating a one-page PDF summary. But this will not be the exact structure of your full pitch deck! This is a teaser of sorts. Create a great blurb that says simply what your startup does. This concise document should include and fit the following key elements:

WHO?
WHAT?
WHY THIS MATTERS?
WHY NOW?
HOW IS YOUR STARTUP DOING? [TRACTION]

Creating a one-sentence elevator pitch can help you arrive at a summary. The one-sentence pitch should be concise and not be more than twenty-five words, as research shows that this is the threshold most people can handle when they read. It should answer the question, "What is the business you are in, and what do you do?" briefly and clearly.

To help you organize your ideas further, taking into consideration the key elements we mentioned, you can adapt this simple anatomy of a value proposition:

[Your Company] _____

with [product/service] _____

which solves [problem] _____

helps _____

[Customers/Users/Consumers] _____

to _____

and is better than anything out there, because [Your Company] _____

with [product/service] _____

which solves [problem] _____

helps [Customers/Users/Consumers] _____

to _____

and is better than anything out there, because [value provided] _____

and [value provided] _____

The answers to these questions below are most likely what investors need to know first. This format can also be a short teaser deck you can send before a first meeting with potential investors. You may use a product like DocSend that requires the reader to enter their email and helps you track how many minutes they spend on each slide.

Although some investors hate this and prefer to get a PDF, if DocSend or a similar tool is common in your market, feel free to use that first.

However, be aware that some investors may use a random or even a "burner" email address to access it. The following should be obvious to the reader of your message and your email can easily follow this format:

- **Problem**: What is the problem you are trying to solve or a need you're trying to address? What is your unique insight?

- **Solution**: How does your product solve the problem in a way that is ten times better than existing solutions? People hate change, so why is this massively different AND better AND who are the crazy, earliest adopters? What kind of business is it? Is this a technology business?

- **Why Now**: Why does the world need this product *today*? With regards to the market feasibility, how big is the market? What is the *serviceable,* and what is the *obtainable* market for your product or service?

- **The Team**: Why is this the best team in the world to win?

- **Traction**: What progress has the business made so far? The information can include your revenues, the number or percentage of products shipped, users who onboarded, and so on.

- **What's Next:** What does this capital unlock and enable you to do at the next level?

Making Your Presentation

For the presentation, using fewer slides, ideally ten to fifteen, is advisable. Create two decks, the first having five to eight slides. This will serve as the aforementioned teaser deck that will be emailed out ahead of the meeting with the VCs.

The second deck is longer and is what you're going to use live in the pitch meeting. It also includes appendices that will serve as extra information to answer any follow-up questions or help you jump to the most relevant topics that come up in your conversations.

Similar to the one-pager, the second deck is more elaborate, with each page expanding on those five topics we mentioned above. It's also recommended that you add a few more slides to introduce the team first.

Your presentation deck generally should include the following details. Assess and evaluate whether your descriptions answer the corresponding questions for each key element:

- **Cover Page**: Provide a clear and simple title.

- **The Team**: Include executive bios in this section. It should answer, "Why is this the best team in the world to win?" The headline should be a clear answer to this question and not the word team.

- **Problem**: What is the problem you are trying to solve? What are your unique insights? Do not make the headline just say "Problem." Use that space to be more insightful.

- **Solution**: How does your product solve the problem in a way that is ten times better than existing solutions? Is this a technology business? What's the secret sauce? Describe that in the headline rather than "bury the lead" in the body of the text on the slide.

- **Why Now**: Why does the world need your product or service today? Capture that as a provocative headline.

- **Market**: How big is the market? What is the serviceable and obtainable market? How fast is it growing? Quantify this in your headline for the greatest impact. (see glossary for definitions of market size)

- **Traction**: What progress have you made so far? Include details on revenues, products shipped, users onboarded, or relevant statistics. Here, write your headline to emphasize one or more metrics that matter to show your growth to date.

- **Competition**: How do you compare your business to the competition by features or business model? What makes your business unique enough? Is it defensible now or in the future? Share an insight you have in your headline about your competition rather than say you don't have any close competition.

- **Ask**: How much are you asking for from investors for this round? It's best to provide a history of prior investments and any notable investors who have participated in your startup. State this numerical figure in your headline.

- **Use of Funds**: What do the next twenty-four to thirty-six months look like? How will you use funds? What are you using the money for that goes beyond existing cash burn? Does this show scrappiness, especially in times of challenges?

- **Additional Financial Data**: Show details of your traction and future milestones for the business.

- **Recap/Summary**: Summarize your business, your strategy, and how much you are raising.

I've mentioned adding some slides to introduce your team. Let me share a quick story related to that. I was working with Mike, who put together a pitch for investors. The focus of the startup was a financial institution that provided people with quality financial guidance so they could make saving money easier.

One of the things I shared was to focus on the team because investors want to back highly rated teams. So, instead of starting with the problem and presenting the solution, he introduced who we are. Doing that helped highlight why they were the ideal people in the world and the team to win.

He also emphasized why they would successfully build this product, which they did with just a little money. As a result, they were able to eventually exit by selling their business to a public company.

Let's Have a Quick Deck Check

To help you check whether you have all the information you need in your presentation, see if you've covered the six T's framework that many VCs use some version of to screen deals:

1. **Team**: Is your team the best in the world to execute this business plan?

2. **Total Addressable Market**: Can this be a unicorn startup with a path to $100-200 million in revenue?

3. **Traction**: Is the business growing exponentially?

4. **Technology**: Is it truly a technology or at least a technology-enabled business? Does the product or service have a defensible competitive advantage?

5. **Trends**: What are the trends of the business? What other businesses compete?

6. **Terms**: How much are you raising? This is important so investors can see if their check would fit with their portfolio strategy.

Maybe you're wondering why you have to create two decks. The point of the PDF teaser deck is to send enough information to get to the first meeting. It's not for them to have every piece of information they could want or need to make the investment. That will be covered in your pitch deck and detailed in the due diligence process.

The point of the PDF or the elevator pitch is to get someone's interest and attention if you need them to make a warm intro.

Caution About NDAs

You've probably heard about asking VCs to sign NDAs during the fundraising process. But here are very important things to consider and why it isn't advisable:

- **VCs and NDAs**: Venture capitalists almost universally do not sign NDAs because ideas are not considered unique or protectable. VCs often hear similar pitches regularly and invest in the team's ability to execute the idea rather than the idea itself. They don't want the headache of dealing with irate founders later because they didn't back their deal. VCs generally don't, and angels usually won't sign NDAs.

For example, you're going to invest in a ride-sharing app, but the problem is that other companies are trying to start a ride-sharing startup. You met with three different companies and are picking this one because it has the strongest traction. What if one of the others signed an NDA with you, and then you invested in someone else? You guessed it. They'll get angry, and most probably, it will lead to a lawsuit. Not convinced? Consider the following:

- **Unsophisticated Signal**: Asking investors to sign an NDA can be perceived as a sign of unsophistication among founders. It may indicate a lack of understanding of the norms and dynamics of the fundraising process.

- **Legal Risks and Practicality**: If multiple investors were to sign NDAs, it could potentially lead to legal complications if any of them choose not to invest but were exposed to similar ideas elsewhere. This scenario could result in accusations of idea theft or breaches of confidentiality.

- **Alternatives to Protecting Information**: Instead of NDAs, founders can take modest steps to protect sensitive information by using secure data rooms where access is controlled and logged. This method ensures that only trusted parties have access to confidential materials and provides a record of who has viewed them.

- **Due Diligence on Investors**: Founders should conduct thorough due diligence on potential investors. This includes researching their portfolio to ensure there are no conflicts of interest or competitive investments that could compromise sensitive information. Don't assume that the investors will not take a meeting with you if you are competitive, as they may feel at the time that it wasn't obvious to them.

- **Open Communication**: During initial discussions with investors, it's prudent for founders to inquire about the investor's current investment focus and recent deployments. This helps gauge their genuine interest and ensures that sensitive information is appropriately shared.

Organizing Your Data Room

Now, let's help you organize your data room. The Data Room for investors has, at a minimum, the long version of the deck plus the following:

- **Latest Cap Table**: This is a description of the ownership of the company, the how, the who, and how many shares they own.

- **Documentation of Past Term Sheets, Safes, or Convertible Notes**

- **Financial Model**: This shows the current projections for the business, providing a pro forma picture of revenues, expenses, profit or loss, and sources and uses of cash, including anticipated cash flow needs.

- **Historical Financial Statements**: This is ideally audited at Series B or C and beyond and includes the balance sheet, income statement, and statement of cash flows.

- **Documentation of Patents and IP**

- **Description of Any Claims, Liens, or Lawsuits Against The Company**

- **Customer Testimonials or Contact Information:** Include customer opt-in and preparation to participate in a due diligence interview.

- If applicable, **Registry of Other Assets** including asset register, list of and value of financial accounts.

- **Executive Bios**

- **List of Advisors and Their Bios**

- **Board of Directors List with Their Bios**

Your data room may also include:

- **Market data and research**

- **Past investor updates**

- **Marketing materials**

- **Proof of insurance (property and Directors and Officers Liability insurance)**

As with teaser decks, DocSend (owned by DropBox), Box, DropBox, and other tools are commonly used for virtual data rooms (VDR). There should be a cloud drive for each investor that you get to do some diligence on, as well as for those who want to look at the data room and see what's there.

Take note that some data rooms may reveal who else is there and what they are looking at. Hence, it makes sense to have a separate or duplicate data room for each investor to look at, especially with information like customer lists, key financials, etc.

Basically, your data room contains nearly all the information that investors will then have to do their due diligence. They may call your customers and find out how strongly they believe in your product and business.

Let's Check If You're Content-Ready

Once you start fundraising, things will be *very* busy, and you won't be able to stop and work on different things like your VDR. I'm reminded of one founder named Diana, who got an enthusiastic response from an investor asking for the VDR that same day.

Don't be flat-footed and miss out. As an entrepreneur, you also need to be content-ready **BEFORE** engaging investors so you won't look unprepared. Investors will likely give a negative perception because they're struggling to understand or start due diligence on your company.

Here's a checklist to help you get organized and ready with your content and what else you need to prepare:

- **Teaser Deck**
- **Meeting Deck**
- **Virtual Data Room**
- **Cap Table Management Tool**
- **Target List of VCs for others to make a warm introduction to you**
- **CRM for Tracking Conversations**

Maya didn't waste time organizing her content, starting from her one-page summary pitch, slide presentations, and data room. She made sure she gathered all the information she needed about her team, information about her company's financial aspects, and pertinent records that would support her startup. She also followed Arya's advice on dismissing the need for an NDA.

Coupled with her earlier assignments on investor research and creating a workable process, everything finally started to fall into place. Now she had some fundraising puzzle pieces together; she only needed the remaining pieces to see the whole final picture.

Chapter 5

Outreach and Engagement

I've had the opportunity to attend different fundraising meetings in my years of experience. Many of those meetings seemed to be full of potential. But sadly, I often hear the "Sound of Silence" play loudly inside my head during these meetings. That's when I learned that fundraising is indeed a skill. It's comparable to sales, hiring, or product design. I've noticed a common mistake among startup founders: they often focus too much on their biography, trying to persuade or impress the investor.

The most important story about you is your ability to learn fast, according to Shawn Xu, partner at Lowercarbon Capital. He says, "Learning velocity paired with a bias to action based on new learnings are the paired green-flag traits I look for in a founder."

Fundraising is about presenting your vision in a way that resonates with you and those who hold the key to your future—the investors.

Additionally, it's crucial to capture the investor's interest by emphasizing the product's market fit, usability, and potential for adoption. Fundraising is a skill that is similar to business development and hiring. What all these have in common is sales. More than mere persuasion, it's about getting a solid buy-in for your vision and business.

Maya had been in this scenario before, a room with venture capitalists she was aiming to win over as her investors. She had flashbacks of that day when she presented InsightAI. Only this time, it was different. After months of doing her homework, listing VCs, preparing and organizing content details and information crucial to her business, she's finally set several appointments. And she knew better, much better, this time.

With Arya's coaching, she knew what she needed to do, arrange, and what she was going to say. She was ready to engage in the conversation and talk serious sense about her startup.

Interrupted with Your Pitch? Ask Questions Back!

Interruptions can work for you! Every interruption is a good sign that people are interested and engaged. If they quietly and politely listen, their mind is probably thinking about what's for lunch or buying the new skis they saw online. So here are some techniques you can apply when faced with interruptions:

- **Ask great questions**: Turn your pitch into a two-way conversation. Remember, this is a long-term partnership, and it's crucial to engage the investor from the start. Use interruptions to your advantage by turning objections into questions and encouraging further discussion.

  When pitching to investors, it's crucial to craft your presentation in an engaging, two-way conversation. Pausing during the presentation to invite questions and insights is incredibly effective. It breaks the monotony and allows investors to share their knowledge and feel involved. For instance, asking them about their insights in the space or any watchouts they might have based on their knowledge of your target segment can be invaluable. VCs love feeling smart and appreciated for their expertise or past experience, and this method taps into that.

- **Engage and involve**: Ask for their insights and experiences. Let them show off their knowledge and pattern-matching skills. This not only makes them feel valued but also provides them with useful information.

  You can say, "Here's what we're doing, but can you also share your experience?" You can also encourage their interruptions by saying, "Should we dig deeper into what you were describing?" Sometimes you might well respond to their questions with questions like, "Can you tell me more about what you mean?"

- **Respond thoughtfully**: When they raise objections or questions, don't immediately agree or change your plans. Instead, thank them for the input, express that you will consider it, and ask for more details or clarification. This reflects in the rigor of your thinking and admitting what you don't know yet but have the ability to figure out with your current plan. Samantha Huang of BMW iVentures explains, "I get suspicious when founders oversell me or answer questions without any logical thinking behind it. My job as a venture capitalist during diligence is to drill down into specific aspects of the business and stress-test founders' assumptions and thought processes. The reality is that while founders should have a good understanding of the fundamentals of their business, I don't expect them to know absolutely everything. I would rather have a founder tell me that he will have to think further about a question and come back to me with a sound answer versus making it up on the spot."

- **Show your depth of knowledge**: Be ready to dive into detailed questions about your financial model and other aspects of your business. Demonstrating a thorough understanding of your numbers and assumptions builds credibility. As Martin

Tobias of Incisive Ventures says, "Solely relying on things like Google ads shows a lack of creativity." Show the rigor of your thinking.

If investors ask detailed questions about your financial model, take the opportunity to demonstrate your deep understanding of your numbers. Be prepared to dive into your assumptions, growth rates, and projections. This shows that you are not only well-prepared but also thoughtful about the twists and turns of your business journey. It's essential to convey to investors that you're focused on building a valuable company, not just meeting short-term inputs like hiring engineers or opening a sales office.

- **Monitor body language**: Be keen about the atmosphere. Take their body language as a reason to engage rather than seeing them just staring blankly. Interrupt their daydream and bring them back. If they seem disengaged, ask if they have any questions or thoughts on the topic. Bring them back into the conversation to regain and maintain their interest.

- **Use rephrasing techniques**: When answering questions, rephrase the question to ensure understanding, provide a concise answer (when in doubt, answer in exactly three parts), and then confirm if the question was answered. This helps keep the conversation clear and ensures mutual understanding.

A technique I learned from a top communications coach is not to ramble because that's how you will lose people. If you only do one thing, rephrase the question and confirm that's what they mean. It's important to get that feedback. This will take practice because you often want to get to the point where you're just so relieved to get through the answer and keep moving or return to your slides.

- **Be adaptable**: If an investor seems particularly interested in a specific part of your pitch, be ready to skip ahead or delve deeper into that section. Flexibility shows that you're responsive and considerate of their interests or concerns.

  You can ask them if they wish to skip to that section, and if they say yes, then jump ahead. You don't have to move sequentially.

  The goal is to maintain control of the conversation, keep the investor engaged, and demonstrate that you're a thoughtful and prepared founder. This approach not only makes for a more dynamic pitch but also lays the foundation for a productive and lasting partnership.

- **Practice your storytelling skills:** Stress that "This is what I've experienced or observed to be true." When you say your experience or your observation, it's hard for them to argue with. That's because you're building a company from your unique insights and experience as opposed to arguing about data or saying this must be true. That's a very important approach in order to be heard well by your investor counterpart.

Remember, these folks are your peers and your future business partners. You should treat them with respect, and they will treat you the same way. But too much deference is a bad thing. You are no less worthy than a VC. You are someone who is going to be the founder and leader of a valuable business, and you are now giving them the opportunity to be a part of that future as an investor.

Ultimately, turning your pitch into a conversation eventually builds a long-term relationship with the investor. It signals to them that you're open to feedback, capable of thoughtful dialogue, and serious about handling the complexities of your business. So, remember to stop, invite questions, and truly engage in the conversation. The remaining section of this chapter will help you manage these conversations.

Investors Invest in Lines and Not Dots

Investors are looking for long-term partnerships. They see their investment as part of a continuous journey rather than a one-time event. When pitching to a VC, you're essentially seeking someone who will be a long-term owner of your business, often for seven, ten years, or even longer.

Some VCs, like the legendary Sequoia Capital, express a desire to hold stakes in high-performing portfolio companies indefinitely, recognizing that substantial value can be realized well beyond the initial public offering. This perspective emphasizes the need to approach these relationships with a partnership mindset rather than an adversarial one.

It's crucial to see your investors as partners for many years to come. This understanding doesn't mean you should blindly agree with everything they suggest, but you should carefully consider whether they will support you through various stages of growth. Will they champion your cause during follow-on rounds? Do they have a reputation that aligns with your long-term vision for the company?

These investors will be linked to your business for a duration that often exceeds the length of many marriages, so it's vital to choose wisely. Before committing, it's essential to understand their ticket size, whether they lead deals, and their follow-on strategy. Ask about their investment process and timeline to see if they align with your goals.

Inform Investors of Your Progress

In engaging with investors, it's essential to demonstrate your progress effectively. As Nuno Goncalves Pedro of Chameleon VC puts it,

"That means show your progress. That does not mean trying things out in front of investors. Be prepared and polished, and know your numbers. They can only invest in what they see before them. Don't make them have to guess or imagine too much, or your deal will be stuck in their investment funnel."

You can regularly send investor updates via email, and using software like Visible can streamline this process. Visible and similar sites offer templates to help you organize and send updates efficiently. Here's a minimal viable example of how you might structure your first updates:

- **Message from the Founder:** A brief note addressing the investors personally.

- **Summary:** A quick overview of what's happening in the company.

- **Wins:** Highlight recent successes and milestones achieved. Thank investors or others who have actively helped (make them look good).

- **Challenges:** Share the obstacles you're facing and how you plan to overcome them.

- **Priorities:** Outline your current focus areas and strategic priorities.

- **Metrics:** Provide key performance indicators that showcase your company's growth and health.

- **Asks:** Indicate how readers can help.

Consistency in communication is key. You might tailor different updates for various audiences: a comprehensive one for current investors and a more concise version for prospective investors. The latter might omit detailed challenges and metrics, focusing on positive progress and high-level achievements. This approach provides enough information to keep interest high without overwhelming them with details that require in-depth diligence.

Finding Out Where Investors Are in Their Fund Life

Part of having conversations with VCs is understanding where that firm is in the lifecycle of its fund. Here are practical steps to help you as a founder to determine this information:

1. Understand Fund Lifecycle Stages

Fund lifecycle stages can be determined in these periods. This step is also crucial when you set the timing to approach VCs:

- **Investment Period:** Typically, in the first three to five years of the fund, the VC actively seeks new investments.

- **Harvesting Period:** The remaining years will be focused on supporting existing investments and seeking exits.

- **Fundraising for the Next Fund:** If the VC is raising their next fund, they might be less focused on new investments from their current fund, even if they have the opportunity to recycle some returns into new deals.

2. Ask Direct Questions

During pitch meetings, ask investors directly about the age of their current fund and how much capital is left for new investments. You can include the following key questions:

- What is the vintage year of your current fund?
- How many investments will you make from the fund?
- How much capital is reserved for follow-on investments?

- Are you currently raising or planning to raise a new fund soon?
- What's your target ownership?

An example question might be: "Can you share more about the stage your current fund is in? Are you actively making new investments or more focused on follow-ons and exits?"

3. Research Publicly Available Information

Current and accurate data is still hard to find. Check the VC firm's website and press releases for announcements about their funds. You can also look at industry reports and databases like PitchBook or Crunchbase, which often provide details on fund sizes and stages. Try also looking into reports from venture capital research firms or industry publications that analyze and provide overviews of VC firm activities and fund lifecycles.

4. Leverage Venture Capital Newsletters

Take time to read VC updates and newsletters regularly. These often contain insights about where the firm is focusing its efforts and any new funds being raised. Sign up for newsletters or follow the VC firm on social media to stay informed about their activities and announcements.

5. Evaluate Their Recent Investments

Look into and analyze the VC firm's recent investments. If they are making a lot of new investments, they are likely in the early stages of their fund. On the other hand, if they are more involved in follow-on rounds or exits, they might be in the later stages.

6. Utilize Networking

Another great way to find out where investors are in their fund lifecycle is to connect with other founders who have raised money from the same VC. They can provide insights into the firm's investment focus and fund lifecycle. Attend industry events and conferences where VCs are speaking or participating. They often discuss their fund status and investment thesis in these settings.

Convincing Investors to Advocate for Your Round

When it comes to your potential investors, it's not just about having a great pitch but also about aligning with what drives their decision-making. When investors are prepared and confident, they are more likely to champion your round in investment committee. This involves several key steps:

- **Understanding What Conviction Looks Like for Investors**
Knowing what makes specific investors confident in a startup is key. This includes understanding their criteria for success and what factors make them willing to advocate for your company. Traction solves all arguments and resolves debates.

- **Asking About the Preparation Needed for Investors to Champion Your Round**
It's essential to inquire directly about what investors need to feel prepared to advocate for your round. This could be detailed financial projections, market analysis, or a strong pitch deck. Doing so also sets clear expectations between you and your investors.

- **Memo Writing: Providing Necessary Information**
Create comprehensive memos that cover your business model, market potential, competitive landscape, and financial health. Having all the necessary data at their fingertips makes it easier for investors to advocate for you. A good fundraiser will send investors a well-written deck. A great fundraiser will be to write a memo for the VC, making the case for why to invest in this company and why now. With that, their work may be half done.

Manage the Meeting

Effectively managing investor meetings can impact the outcome of your fundraising efforts. It's about steering the conversation, understanding their needs, and ensuring they have everything they need to move forward confidently.

1. Ask What's Next

Always ask about the next steps and who will be involved in the process. Understanding the path to the investment committee and what is needed for a close will help you manage the process efficiently.

2. Explore the Thesis Fit of Your Business

As mentioned in Chapter 2, you will be looking for what it takes for investors to have conviction in your round. This might involve creating detailed memos or providing additional information that makes them feel confident advocating for your startup. Create that FOMO. It's the fear of missing out that will drive their decision-making.

Here's the principle: Make an observation from their portfolio, thesis, or social media, tie it back to your startup, and then ask, "Did I understand that correctly?"

A powerful way to engage investors is to show that you've done your homework. Observe their portfolio, investment thesis, or social media activity, and relate it to your startup. This demonstrates that you understand their interests and how your startup fits into their strategy.

3. Be Influential

I'd like to borrow Dr. Robert Cialdini's Principles of Persuasion[4] and put it in the context of fundraising. From these points, you can

---

[4] Robert Cialdin, "Seven Principles of Persuasion," Influence at Work, https://www.influenceatwork.com/7-principles-of-persuasion/

drive additional ideas on how you can further improve in engaging investors:

- **Reciprocity**: Show that you have done something for them first by deeply understanding their interests and sharing something insightful.

- **Scarcity**: Highlight the unique opportunity and how they might miss if they don't invest now.

- **Authority**: Establish yourself as an expert in your field.

- **Consistency**: People want to appear consistent with their past statements and actions so reference them.

- **Liking**: Build rapport and establish a personal connection, based on shared interests and background.

- **Social Proof:** Show that others are already backing your product or company.

- **Unity**: Demonstrate that you share common values and goals.

There's an art of influence in storytelling that can get people hooked. It's a powerful communication skill that you'll be able to develop in the long run. Use it in your presentations as you meet with different VCs. Along the way, you will want to signal your ability to keep learning and iterating. With every time you practice, you'll become more natural and confident to engage investors in a conversation.

Chapter 6

Understanding Term Sheets and Cap Tables

Maya is now on top of her game, meeting with VCs and presenting InsightAI. She remembered how she struggled to understand the specifics of term sheets and cap tables. It took her a while to grasp the process and weigh negotiations to her advantage. With the help of experienced peers and initial advice as she started to vet lawyers, the weeks of exploring and learning this important aspect of fundraising paid off.

Like many fields, you can expect a lot of jargon in fundraising. Founders new to fundraising often find terms and document details intimidating simply because they were designed by lawyers or bankers. And just like Maya, you can be overwhelmed at the start. That's understandable. But it ultimately comes down to a few questions of arithmetic and a little algebra to know what's left for you vs. others. It's also about how you can push for a clean term sheet that doesn't leave you in an adverse situation.

As a founder, you need to have a clear understanding of what Term Sheets and Cap Tables (Capitalization Tables) are and the specific terms and details included in these agreements and tables. This is crucial not only to secure your funding but also to shape the trajectory of your company during the early stages.

Term Sheets, for instance, go beyond legalities. Do not just consider them a formality of accepting capital. These agreements serve as the foundational framework for your partnership with investors. They detail essential aspects like valuation, investment terms, and governance, setting the stage for a productive relationship. Mastery of these details can mean the difference between a successful funding round and potential challenges down the road. Similarly, Cap Tables are indispensable tools for understanding equity distribution among stakeholders.

This chapter is an introduction to term sheets and cap tables, along with details and essential terms you, as a founder, need to be familiar with. These topics are too important to leave to your lawyer to understand and not you. If you'd like to see an example of a vanilla term sheet, check out several link in the Additional Resources Section.

Key Elements of a Term Sheet

Let's start with a simple definition of a term sheet. A term sheet is a non-binding agreement establishing the basic terms and conditions under which an investment will be made. It serves as a template to develop more detailed legally binding documents, typically created by lawyers retained by the investors (and the legal fees charged to the new portfolio company). You will also need legal counsel.

You can model your own term sheet in a few places, including on the Wilson Sonsini website (https://ecp.wsgr.com/generators/term-sheet-generator). They're one of the most prominent law firms there, but remember to consult your lawyer before using a term sheet. To further grasp the use and significance of a term sheet, let's look into some financial terms you'll encounter and the main components of this document.

Key Financial Terms
- **Amount Raised and Valuation**

The amount raised refers to the total funds sought by a startup from investors in a particular financing round. This figure is crucial as it directly impacts the company's financial runway and operational capabilities. Valuation, on the other hand, determines the pre-money worth of the company before the investment or may be expressed post-money (after new funds are received). It plays a pivotal role in determining the equity stake investors receive in exchange for their capital, influencing the overall terms and conditions of the investment deal.

- **Price per Share**

The price per share specifies the valuation at which investors acquire ownership in the company. This price is determined based on various factors, including the company's financial performance, market conditions, and investor expectations. This serves as a critical metric in calculating the financial terms of the investment, such as the equity percentage acquired by investors and the overall capital raised by the company.

- **Rights of Shareholders**

The rights of shareholders encompass a range of privileges and protections granted to individuals who hold equity in a company. These rights typically include voting rights in corporate decisions, information access regarding company operations and financial performance, and protections against dilution of their ownership stake. Shareholder rights are outlined in the company's bylaws and shareholder agreements, ensuring transparency, accountability, and fairness in corporate governance practices. If receiving preferred stock, the share may not contain the same voting provisions and will be senior in the "preference stack," meaning it will be paid back before common stock.

- **Use of Proceeds**

The use of proceeds may outline how the funds raised from investors will be allocated within the company. It provides clarity on the intended purposes of the capital infusion, such as funding product development initiatives, expanding market reach through marketing efforts, covering operational expenses, or pursuing strategic acquisitions. Proper allocation of proceeds is essential for achieving the company's growth objectives while maximizing shareholder value and ensuring efficient capital deployment.

Components of a Term Sheet

A term sheet serves as a foundational document outlining an investment's preliminary terms and conditions, paving the way for more detailed legal agreements. Here's a detailed breakdown of its essential components based on my experience and insights:

- **Securities Issued**

The term sheet specifies the type of securities issued to investors, whether common shares, preferred shares, or convertible instruments like SAFEs or convertible notes. Each type of security carries distinct rights and preferences, impacting both investor returns and control dynamics within the company. For example, if we're raising $1 million and issuing shares, we need to clearly state the number of shares and the corresponding price per share. When receiving capital in a priced round, typically Series A or later, convertible preferred shares are received by the VCs.

- **Valuation Methods**

Valuation methods outlined in the term sheet establish the company's worth at the time of investment. This valuation determines the pricing of shares or the conversion terms for convertible securities, influencing the equity stake acquired by investors and the overall financial terms of the deal. For instance, if the valuation is set at $10 million and we're raising $1 million by issuing shares, the price per share would reflect this valuation. This should clearly be explained as either the pre-money or post-money valuation (with or without the new expected capital).

- **Rights and Preferences**

Rights and preferences include critical provisions such as liquidation preferences, which dictate the order in which proceeds are distributed in the event of a sale or liquidation. Anti-dilution provisions protect investors from equity dilution caused by subsequent rounds of financing, ensuring their initial investment retains its value over time. This might involve terms that allow investors to maintain their ownership percentage in future funding rounds.

- **Conversion Terms**

As mentioned earlier, convertible instruments like convertible notes or SAFEs, conversion terms specify when and how these debts will convert into equity. These terms provide flexibility in structuring early-stage investments while deferring the valuation discussion until a future financing round or milestone event. For example, a convertible note might convert into equity at a 20 percent discount during the next qualified financing round. Alternatively, it may contain a cap (not to be confused with your cap table), which places a maximum valuation or "cap" at which the equity will convert. This rewards early-stage risk takers who have bet on your company by allowing them to convert their note or SAFE into equity at a potentially lower price than the new investors receive. This is favorable for investors but not necessarily for the founders. Model this across a few scenarios in a spreadsheet before accepting those terms from an investor.

- **Investor Protections**

Investor protections outlined in the term sheet may include registration rights, granting investors the ability to request registration of their shares for public sale, and information rights. This ensures transparency by providing access to the company's financial and operational updates. In addition, investors are kept informed and can act if necessary to protect their investment.

- **Governance and Control**

Governance provisions detail board seats and voting rights granted to investors, influencing decision-making processes within the company. These provisions are crucial for aligning investor interests with strategic initiatives and maintaining balance in corporate governance. For instance, a lead investor might be given a seat on the board to have a say in major company decisions.

- **Employee Stock Options Pool**

The term sheet typically allocates a portion of the company's equity for employee stock options, incentivizing key talent and aligning their interests with long-term company success. This pool is essential for attracting and retaining skilled employees in competitive markets. For example, it might state that 10–20 percent of the company's shares are reserved for this purpose.

- **Legal and Tax Considerations**

Legal and tax considerations encompass provisions such as Qualified Small Business Stock (QSBS) treatment, which can offer tax benefits to investors and founders upon exiting their investment. Additionally, the allocation of legal fees and responsibilities between the company and investors is clarified to ensure fair and efficient legal representation throughout the transaction process. For instance, the term sheet might specify that the company receiving the investment will cover up to $50,000 in legal fees related to the funding transaction.

- **No-Shop Clause and Governing Law**

A no-shop clause restricts the company from soliciting alternative investment offers during the due diligence and investment finalization period with the current investors. While the term sheet itself may not be legally binding, this clause is, in fact, binding.

This means that once we sign off on a term sheet and you (my lead investor) are ready to invest a million dollars in my startup, I can't turn around and use that offer to negotiate better terms or higher valuations from other venture capitalists. I can't go to another VC and say, "Hey, I'm getting $1 million from person A. Will you give me $2 million?" or "Can you offer me a better valuation?" This clause ensures that the currently *accepted* deal is exclusive and prevents me from shopping around for a better deal once we've agreed on the initial terms.

If investors discover I'm shopping the term sheet around, they could justifiably pull the offer, undermining the entire funding round. Though a term sheet is a non-binding commitment, it's still a promise to negotiate in good faith. For example, you might be leading the round with your investment, which doesn't preclude other investors from joining under the same terms, but I must stop looking for alternative or better terms once we've accepted and signed the term sheet.

Another component of the term sheet includes the governing law clause, which specifies the jurisdiction whose laws will govern the interpretation and enforcement of the term sheet and subsequent legal agreements. For example, many startups opt for Delaware law due to its business-friendly environment and established case law for nearly all matters, even if they operate elsewhere, like California or New York. This needs to be specified as well in the term sheet.

There are more other components in a term sheet but basically, these are the most important ones you must keep an eye on.

Importance of Cap Tables

Now, let's talk about cap tables. The Cap Table (capitalization table) is a formal spreadsheet or table that shows the capitalization for a company and by whom. That means it lists all company securities such as common equity shares, preferred equity shares, SAFE or convertible notes, warrants (rights to purchase shares), and who owns them. This is sometimes shown on a fully diluted basis, so imagine that all securities are converted into common stock.

You need to understand who owns, who controls, and who runs your business and how possible scenarios for financing can change all that without you knowing how that might be possible. You also need to have a clear understanding of the governance of the corporation, how you run your business, and how much of it you, as a founder, are left with.

Structure and Format

The structure of a cap table typically includes columns for different types of securities, the names of the holders, the number of shares or options held, and the percentage of total ownership. It may also include the potential ownership assuming full conversion of all securities into common stock. For example, at the current moment, management might own only common shares, while employees hold stock options that give them the right to buy shares in the future. When an exit event occurs, like an acquisition or IPO, all convertible securities, whether a SAFE or convertible preferred stock, usually convert to common stock, providing a complete picture of ownership for payout purposes.

Today, we can utilize specialized cap table management tools like Carta, Figure, or Pulley. These products streamline the process, allowing you to input ownership data categorized by type of equity (common stock, preferred stock, options), owner (founder, investor class), and issuance date. This level of detail and organization is invaluable for future reference.

How to Negotiate

1. Strategies for Effective Negotiation

Negotiating a term sheet is a critical skill for any startup founder. The goal is to secure investment while maintaining as much ownership and control as possible. Here are key strategies to equip you to negotiate with investors effectively:

2. Understand Your BATNA (Best Alternative to a Negotiated Agreement)

Before signing a term sheet, leverage your BATNA by exploring multiple investment opportunities. Inform potential investors you have a term sheet but haven't signed it yet. Before signing a term sheet, explore other potential investors and see if you can bring in additional investors as co-investors. This can strengthen your negotiating position and potentially lead to better terms. Your BATNA isn't to raise money or die trying or even raise or bootstrap, but it is a set of options that get you to your goal.

3. Know Market Terms

Familiarize yourself with common market terms and how frequently they appear in current deals. Terms like the Right of First Refusal (ROFR), drag-along rights, and participating preferred shares might not be common but can appear. Understanding their prevalence and implications helps you decide whether to accept or push back on such terms. Some of these deals may be exploding offers, but the VC bias for FOMO may bring more potential lead investors to the table in a short time who will offer a term sheet to you.

4. Seek Legal Counsel

Engage an attorney with experience in the current market trends. Your legal counsel can guide you on whether specific terms are standard or unusual, helping you avoid unfavorable conditions. As the saying goes, "You are never too rich to afford a cheap lawyer." This may be especially true in Silicon Valley, where using an inexperienced law firm signals a lack of sophistication and awareness of risks to your investors. Again, err on the side of experience and build a trusted relationship with your law firm.

5. Assess Investor Value Beyond Capital

Evaluate whether a potential investor can provide more than just funds. Consider their experience in your industry, past investments in similar companies, and recommendations from other founders.

A valuable investor offers strategic guidance and support that goes beyond financial investment. Have they invested in similar companies before? Can they provide strategic guidance and support? Do other founders in their portfolio recommend them? These factors are crucial in choosing the right investor for your business.

6. Negotiate Key Terms
Focus on critical terms such as valuation, control, liquidation preferences, and board composition. Understand how these terms will affect your ownership, control, and the company's future.

7. Take Your Time
Avoid rushing into decisions. Give yourself enough time to evaluate offers and consult with advisors thoroughly. Making a well-informed decision is crucial, as unwinding a funding arrangement is complex and costly. Effective negotiation also entails being clear about your company's needs and long-term vision. It's essential at this time to balance raising enough capital to grow the business while minimizing the dilution of your ownership.

Common Pitfalls to Avoid

Many startup founders often fall into these common pitfalls during the negotiation process. It's best to avoid the following and spare yourself the regrets later.

- **Giving Away Too Much Equity Too Early**

One of the major pitfalls in negotiating term sheets is giving away too much equity too early. This mistake can lead to significant dilution, reducing your ownership stake in the company and potentially undermining your control and motivation. Future investors might be deterred by a cap table that shows the founders own too little of the company.

What's too much? It depends on the math described above. But hypothetically, you may need to give up 5–10 percent at pre-seed, another 10–20 percent at seed, and again, 10–20 percent at Series A. Ideally, the founders should own the majority of the company after a Series A, even accounting for a 10–20 percent option pool to attract employers. However, this is subjective based on the capital raised, the attractiveness of the sector, the eagerness of investors to join the round, and the recent deals in your market.

- **Messy Cap Table**

A "messy" cap table, characterized by numerous small ownership stakes with different pro-rata rights and convertible notes, can complicate future financing rounds. Investors often prefer a "clean" cap table with fewer, more substantial ownership stakes to avoid complications in future investment rounds.

- **Not Understanding Key Terms**

Failing to fully understand the implications of various terms, such as liquidation preferences or anti-dilution provisions, can significantly negatively impact the value of your shares and control over the company. It's crucial to educate yourself on these terms or consult with a knowledgeable advisor.

- **Lack of Strategic Planning**

Being opportunistic when it comes to fundraising without a deliberate and strategic approach can result in unfavorable financing conditions. For instance, repeatedly raising money without a clear strategy can lead to raising too much capital with lots of dilution for you and little traction for investors. This was true in 2021 for some startups. It may also result in a cap table that makes your business less attractive to future investors.

- **Rushing into Decisions**

Rushing to accept the first term sheet you receive without considering other offers can lead to suboptimal decisions. Take your time to receive and evaluate multiple offers, if possible, and compare them to determine which aligns best with your goals in terms of valuation, control, and other key terms. Make sure you also have enough time to evaluate all aspects of the term sheet and consult with advisors before making a decision. No reasonable investor wants founders to agree to terms that are poorly understood. Once the deal is signed, it's difficult for all sides to unwind the arrangement without significant cost and effort.

- **Failing to Use Experienced Legal Counsel**

As mentioned, skipping legal counsel to save costs can be a false economy. Experienced legal counsel can help you understand market terms, provide guidance based on current trends, and ensure that the term sheet you sign is fair and standard without unusual provisions that could harm you in the long run. There's plenty written elsewhere on participating preferred drag-along rights and rachets that form the kind of investor-favorable terms you may never encounter. Still, it's best to have basic knowledge of these or at least be able to spot them.

A Caveat on the Role of Legal Counsel

Having experienced legal counsel, as described above, is invaluable during your term sheet negotiations, as we have pointed out. A good lawyer can help you understand complex terms and ensure that the agreement is fair and meets market standards. They can identify red flags and negotiate on your behalf to secure better terms. Legal counsel also provides the necessary expertise to help you look into the status of legal and tax considerations and legal fee allocations. *However, it's essential not to rely solely on your lawyer.*

As a founder, you must also educate yourself and be actively involved in the negotiation process (*Venture Deals* by Brad Feld and Jason Mendelson is an excellent detailed source to go beyond this book). This dual approach ensures that you make informed decisions and avoid being blindsided by terms you don't fully understand.

As mentioned before, founders may be surprised to learn that their investors' legal fees for a Series A will be paid by them. It's worth re-emphasizing that you should make sure to set a cap on joint legal fees (e.g., $50,000 for a Series A) and take steps to communicate directly with the lead investor. This will shortcut communications, avoid expenses back and forth between lawyers, and allow you to set expectations or terms with the lead investor more confidently, as described by Matt Mochary's book in another excellent reference for founders, *The Great CEO Within*.

Maintaining Ownership and Control

One of the key aspects of negotiating a term sheet is ensuring you retain significant ownership and control of your company. Raising as much money as needed can help maintain a higher ownership stake. Moreover, the more money raised, the greater the expected value of the business in the future. Founders might consider more conservative growth strategies rather than raise a large war chest for a "land grab" if they feel they can partially fund existing revenue and cash flow and minimize reliance on external funding.

Additionally, negotiating special voting stock or board seats can help maintain control. This has become more common since the example of Facebook and Google creating dual-class shares became well-known. For instance, founders might retain shares that carry multiple votes per share or secure conditions that allow them to stay in key leadership roles. Understanding and negotiating these aspects are crucial to staying in the driver's seat as your company grows.

Fully Diluted vs. Current Ownership

Fully diluted ownership reflects what the equity stakes would be if all convertible securities and preferred stock were converted into common stock. This differs from current ownership, which only accounts for currently issued and outstanding shares. Knowing both is essential for accurate financial analysis and planning.

For instance, continuously issuing convertible notes without considering their eventual conversion can lead to significant dilution. This dilution can affect not only the founder's motivation but also the attractiveness of the company to future investors because less ownership by the management often creates less incentive to create outsized value for shareholders. By understanding and negotiating the terms of dilution, founders can better manage their ownership and control over the company.

Chapter 7

Investor Psychology

Fundraising for a startup is like a strategic game of chess. Each move must be carefully planned to secure investment. Just as in chess, understanding the other side's thinking and anticipating their moves is crucial. In fundraising, this means understanding how investors think and leveraging that to your advantage.

In your opening moves, you may well establish credibility and demonstrate potential, akin to controlling the center of the chessboard. As you progress to the middle game, focus on building momentum and creating a sense of urgency, capitalizing on investors' Fear of Missing Out (FOMO), as explained below. Every strategic decision, from showcasing progress to engaging lead investors, parallels a calculated chess move, all aimed at achieving the ultimate goal: securing funding.

Investors Invest Based on FOMO

Investors often operate on the fear of missing out. This term describes their anxiety about missing blockbuster investment opportunities that others might capitalize on. When a lead investor expresses interest in a deal, others may feel they are missing out and become more inclined to invest.

Giving the sense that the "train is leaving the station" can significantly increase investor interest. Investors are motivated by scarcity. They want the deal they can't have, making them more eager to participate if they perceive the opportunity might slip away.

The Importance of Momentum

Momentum is crucial in fundraising. Investors want to see trends and consistent progress. When a startup demonstrates significant momentum, it signals to investors that the company is moving forward and gaining traction, which can increase their interest and willingness to invest. Investors are also more likely to commit when they see that others are already on board, creating a bandwagon effect where interest from one investor can lead to increased interest from others.

I have seen investors ask founders raising their first institutional round (round of capital from funds and entities) who else is in the round. This action is often done because they want to be the last money. Usually, investors will tell a founder how strongly they like what they are doing but ask them to return when they have a lead. Sometimes, once they have a lead, founders find that these investors are willing to take a second look (although some still will not invest anyway as something new has caught their eye).

There was once a founder named Sandy, who spent most of the year fundraising only to find that everyone wanted to follow rather than lead the round. She had more than $10 million circled on paper, but in reality, they had nothing. Once she did have a hint of a lead, it seemed like other investors were suddenly reaching out to try to join the round. Momentum is everything.

Examples of FOMO-Driven Investment Behavior

How does FOMO work for investors? It's based on the idea of scarcity, as mentioned above. Why? Scarcity, it turns out, can be very influential, as Robert Cialdini pointed out in his psychology research, described earlier.

At first, they wonder what they missed. What are the terms of the investment? If the valuation is high or lower than the median valuation at the time. They want to know if this fits with their investment strategy to write a specific, consistent check size at a valuation that gets them their target ownership, which might be 5–7 percent for an accelerator, 10 percent for a seed fund, or even 10–20 percent for others that are multi-strategy funds.

These can be observed in the following investment behaviors:

Party Rounds: As mentioned earlier, these occur when multiple investors contribute smaller amounts to a round, often without a clear lead investor. This behavior was particularly prevalent during the height of the zero-interest rate environment in 2020–2021, where the average number of investors per round peaked.

Waiting for a Lead: As we know now, many investors express interest but prefer to wait until a lead investor is secured before committing. This can leave founders in a position where they appear to have significant interest but lack actual commitments until a lead is confirmed. This leads to a stalemate situation for some founders, who need to show significant commitments to get any interest.

Chasing Hot Deals: Investors often flock to deals that appear to be gaining traction quickly, driven by the fear of missing out on a potentially high-return investment. This behavior can be seen when a startup suddenly gains momentum, prompting a surge of investor interest.

The "Unspoken" No

In fundraising, a "soft" no or "unspoken" no is a rejection that isn't often directly communicated. Instead of saying "No" outright, investors may use vague language or avoid giving a clear response. This move can be frustrating for founders, as it leaves uncertainty about the investor's true intentions.

Understanding the "soft" no is crucial as it helps entrepreneurs to read between the lines and recognize when an investor is not genuinely interested. This type of response often allows investors to keep their options open without committing or providing negative feedback.

Investors often use certain phrases to signal disinterest without explicitly rejecting a pitch. Recognizing these phrases can save founders time and effort. These phrases usually indicate that the investor is not ready to commit or interested in the current opportunity.

Common signals include, but are not limited to the following:

- "You are too early."
- "You are too late."
- "Let's circle back after [a future event or time]."
- "I'm very busy supporting existing portfolio companies."
- "I don't know if this is something my partners are ready for yet."

Distinguishing between a "soft" no and genuine interest is essential. Investors who are genuinely interested typically ask detailed questions about the business, show enthusiasm about the market opportunity, and discuss the next steps in a clear and structured manner. They may also offer to introduce the founders to other investors or resources.

If an investor is vague or avoids discussing specifics, they are likely not genuinely interested. Entrepreneurs should look for clear signs of interest, such as scheduling follow-up meetings or requesting additional information.

Importance of Consistent Updates ("Investing in Lines; Not Dots")

Investors often invest in patterns, observing progress over time rather than making decisions based on a single interaction. This approach is referred to as "investing in lines; not dots," where investors track the startup's trajectory through consistent updates. Regularly updating potential investors on progress, milestones, and achievements keeps them informed and engaged. It helps build a relationship and keeps the startup at the top of mind when the investor is ready to make decisions. Consistent updates demonstrate reliability, transparency, and momentum.

Samantha Huang, principal at BMW iVenture and Head of Content and Board Member at the Emerging Venture Capitalists Association, shares the long-term perspective of many Corporate Venture Capital investors, "I track founders over long periods of time, from months to years. When I catch up with a founder, and I see him or her hitting the benchmarks that they said they would hit from our last meeting, I am positively impressed."

Strategies to Handle and Move On from an "Unspoken" No

Getting unspoken no's is a common experience among founders. So, don't give up. There are ways to handle this and build on your next pitches.

1. **Seek Clarification.** If you suspect a "soft" no, ask the investor directly about their process and what the next steps should be. This can help clarify their level of interest.

2. **Stay Cordial and Professional.** Keep interactions positive and professional, even if you suspect disinterest. Maintaining a good relationship can be beneficial for future opportunities.

3. **Keep Them Updated.** Offer to add the investor to your update emails. This keeps them informed of your progress and can potentially reignite their interest later on. Tailor your updates to different audiences: followers/media, customers, current investors, and potential investors.

4. **Move On and Focus Elsewhere.** Don't dwell on the "soft" no. Focus your efforts on investors who show genuine interest and engagement. Continuously reaching out to new investors and expanding your network increases your chances of finding the right partners.

5. **Learn and Iterate.** Use the feedback, even if indirect, to improve your pitch and approach. Understanding why an investor might not be interested can help refine your strategy for future pitches. Caveat: Feedback on product or go-to-market should taken with a grain of salt unless the GP is a former operator in your space and still understands it well.

Raising Outside Silicon Valley

Raising funds outside of Silicon Valley presents distinct challenges. The number of true, professional venture capital investors in these markets is generally lower, and some may be somewhat less familiar with the high-risk nature of tech startups and "market" investment terms. Non-Silicon Valley regions often lack the same density of networking opportunities and established startup ecosystems. This results in longer fundraising timelines and potentially lower valuations compared to Silicon Valley. Furthermore, the smaller and tighter-knit communities in these regions mean rumors and reputations can spread quickly, influencing investor decisions.

This is not without its drawbacks. Jonathan Charles of Samsung Catalyst Fund says there is a difference in the ability to raise from "smart money." He maintains, "It's not only the amount of dollars that can be raised, but from who." He adds, "Without quality investors around the table, the probability of success is dramatically reduced. This can be as simple as quality 'smart money' investors having a network of people to draw upon that can help or even work in the startup."

Differences in Investor Behavior and Valuations

Investors outside Silicon Valley tend to be more conservative and less likely to be swayed by current trends or fads. While Silicon Valley investors might jump from one hot sector to another, such as generative AI or Web 3.0, investors elsewhere often prioritize stability and long-term viability. They may also be more collaborative, often knowing each other well within their smaller ecosystems, which can lead to a more cohesive investment environment.

However, because these markets have fewer VCs, even significant hubs like Boston or New York still represent only a fraction of the overall investment activity seen in Silicon Valley. These hubs create supportive environments where startups can thrive by offering access to resources, talent, and investors.

In many non-Silicon Valley markets, especially outside the US, government and corporate venture capital play significant roles. Government-backed initiatives and funds provide crucial early-stage financing and support, especially in regions where private venture capital is less prevalent. Corporate Venture Capital (CVC) also plays a key role, with large corporations investing in startups to drive innovation and gain strategic advantages.

In some markets, sovereign wealth funds, government grants, and corporate investments are essential sources of funding, offering stability and long-term support. However, these sources might come with specific requirements or strategic interests aligned with the investors.

Market Dynamics/Ecosystem

Understanding market dynamics is crucial for startups seeking funding. Market dynamics include the forces influencing investor behavior, valuation trends, and the overall investment climate. These forces can vary significantly between regions, so startup strategies vary, and founders need to adapt for successful fundraising.

Silicon Valley is often seen as the epicenter of startup activity in the US. However, other US regions are emerging as significant players, driven by a shift in the investment landscape. According to the "Rise of the Rest" 2023 annual report, regions outside traditional tech hubs are seeing increased investment activity and startup success[5].

Outside the US, markets such as Europe, Southeast Asia, and Latin America have unique dynamics. For example, Europe has a mix of mature and emerging markets from West to East with a deep pool of technical talent, Southeast Asia and India boast rapidly growing digital economies, and Latin America has experienced a surge in fintech and e-commerce startups in recent years.

Government and economic factors also play a significant role in shaping the venture capital landscape, especially outside the US. In many international markets, government and corporate venture capital are critical sources of funding. Sovereign wealth funds, government grants, and corporate investments often have a more substantial presence than in the US, where private venture capital

---

[5] "Shifting Landscapes"—Rise of the Rest's 2023 Annual Report, https://blog.revolution.com/shifting-landscapes-rise-of-the-rests-2023-annual-report-a7bf8427f141

is more dominant. These entities may prioritize strategic interests and long-term stability over short-term returns.

Additionally, the maturity of the venture capital ecosystem varies, with smaller funds often being unable to support a large number of deals or write big checks, leading to a preference for following other investors rather than leading rounds. One may also need to raise some money early and scale without additional capital in certain emerging markets, as downstream capital often may not exist yet, and international investors are not active in that market. This also affects the chances of an exit as there are not likely to be many local acquirors or public capital markets where an IPO is possible.

Chapter 8

Closing with Confidence

There's still one hurdle for Maya to conquer: closing a round with a group of VCs. After weeks of checking in on the investors, asking pertinent questions, communicating several times, and following up, she was now waiting to receive the funding from the solid "yes" she got from the VC firm a few months ago. In the interim, she did more research on the investors.

As Elizabeth Yin of Hustle Fund recommends, "Before you commit to the wrong person, conduct investor reference calls before you accept their offer. You can find references by asking the investor directly, searching on LinkedIn, and asking the people you've talked to for other references."

Maya's tenacious team was also all-out with their support and diligence. She made sure that she would have support. They checked every detail and ensured communication lines were efficient and clear. The lead VC informed her they would email Maya during the week about the round startup and confirm when she would get their wire.

Suddenly, there came the sound of an email notification. It was from the lead firm. Her face lit up as she read the details. Yes, she closed the funding with her VC investor and did it confidently.

Your Process Is Not Over

The deal is not done until the check clears the bank. And the way to get this deal sealed is through a confident close in your fundraising journey. *Closing with confidence means having everything you need to move past negotiations and into the final signatures and wire transfers.*

At this stage, you have all the details of the syndicate investors in the current round, and you have provided them with instructions on what will happen. Prepare a checklist and follow up with reminders, especially if this is an angel round, as the angel investors will operate more slowly at closing times than VCs, whose sole focus is on the business of deploying capital into new investments and may have a formalized process.

People sometimes think, "Okay, great, I sent everything out," but then *they don't follow up* with certain people who expressed interest and even some who committed. You have got to remind people of the round, tell them this is indeed happening, and tell them this is the date it closes. You might need to check in again, ask them any questions, and make sure they have everything they need from you.

"Overcommunicating" often and clearly is key to ensuring everyone is on the same page. The timeline and expectations must be clearly communicated to avoid any surprises.

Strategies for Effective Closing

This may be a very stressful time for you. To ensure a smooth and successful closing process, it's vital for you as a founder to employ strategies that enhance communication and coordination among all parties involved.

1. **Communication**: Always email investors and follow up with a friendly and respectful call or text message if you don't receive a clear acknowledgment. This ensures that important information is received and understood, preventing miscommunication or delays. Track your last communications in whatever spreadsheet or CRM you use to follow up with investors.

2. **Team Coordination**: Copy all the members of the team that you have engaged with at the VC firm to ensure nothing is missed. Double-check that their due diligence process has actually concluded! This keeps everyone informed and allows for a collaborative approach to resolving any issues that can arise.

3. **Preparation**: Create a detailed checklist that you share with another member of your team (e.g., a co-founder) to ensure accountability. This helps keep track of tasks and deadlines, ensuring that all necessary steps are completed in a timely and efficient manner.

4. **CEO Involvement**: As the CEO, you should be set to stay involved in both the pitch and the closing to ensure everything runs smoothly. Your leadership and oversight are crucial in maintaining momentum and addressing any last-minute concerns. Ensuring that your business is sufficiently capitalized is a fundamental responsibility of a CEO.

Common Mistakes in the Closing Process

Many startups falter during the closing process due to common mistakes, which can have long-term consequences if not addressed properly. One major pitfall is assuming that seasoned investors are always organized and have sound administrative systems in place. While investors may be skilled at picking investments, they may struggle with the day-to-day organization of their firms. This is even more true for angel investors who may have a day job that preoccupies their time, making it crucial for you to provide proactive administrative support.

Regular communication and updates are essential to keep the process on track and ensure all parties are aligned. Additionally, don't be afraid to manage your investors and provide clear direction and expectations. Investors often appreciate guidance and clarity about what they need to do and when they need to do it, which can facilitate a smoother closing process.

Here are practical ways you can avoid unnecessary assumptions and ensure your closing is successful:

1. Understand Investor Needs

Ask your investors what they need and what their process is to identify any unique circumstances. Understanding their specific requirements can help you tailor your approach and avoid potential delays. For example, they need to conduct a capital call, get a line, or access funds from a bank pending capital call from their LPs.

2. Anticipate Delays

Identify potential delays, such as moving funds from overseas or getting money out of trust. Being aware of these factors in advance allows you to plan accordingly and mitigate any risks.

3. Communicate Timing

Be aware of timing, schedules, and events that might affect the closing process. Keeping track of critical dates and deadlines ensures you can coordinate effectively with all parties involved. Check bank holidays or major events, especially if investors are out of the country.

4. Stay Informed

Keep track of all the details of your investors' processes to avoid any surprises. Maintaining open lines of communication and staying informed about their progress can help ensure a smooth and successful closing. You can also take note of major events or things they're doing, like building a house or spending holidays with their family as, like it or not, personal circumstances can interrupt your plans.

Clean Cap Tables

As discussed earlier, ensuring a clean cap table before finalizing deals or investments is a crucial phase in fundraising. Things not disclosed in your data room can now become a showstopper at the closing.

Reminder: A cap table lists all the company's securities, including equity shares, convertible notes, SAFEs (Simple Agreements for Future Equity), and other ownership stakes. This table provides a clear picture of who owns what and the implications of their ownership. Sharing the cap table in your data room before due diligence is crucial. As discussed, investors need to thoroughly understand the ownership structure and its implications.

Any ambiguity in the cap table can create uncertainty, making investors hesitant to finalize deals. Different interpretations of fully diluted ownership, multiple SAFEs, convertible notes, or terms triggering new share issuance can cause investors to back out of the round towards the end.

I once worked on an investment in a data services company as part of an angel syndicate with multiple convertible notes, some of which were very short-term and had passed their expiration dates. The company hadn't yet conducted a priced round and hadn't figured out how to roll over or renegotiate the expired notes.

Despite this, they were out raising capital on new notes, including from investors like us. Bottom line: The cap table didn't tell the whole story. The uncertainty surrounding the convertible notes and the overall cap table made it difficult to move forward confidently. This underscores the importance of having an unambiguous cap table. The company must explain what is happening, to whom, and when to maintain investor trust and ensure a smooth investment process.

Chapter 9

Takeaways for Founders

Maya saw a text message from Arya: "Remember, no one will ever see all the things you did below the surface of the iceberg, but be proud of all the steps you took to get here."

As we wrap up, let's have a recap of the key elements that form the backbone of a successful fundraising strategy. The key parts are **Storytelling, Outreach, Organization, and Closing**. This comprehensive framework is designed to be mutually exclusive and collectively exhaustive, covering all crucial aspects of the fundraising process. These principles can help you navigate the complexities of startup funding with confidence and clarity.

Deciding on Types of Funding

The first step in your fundraising journey is deciding on the type of funding that best suits your business needs. Whether bootstrapping, angel investing, venture capital, or crowdfunding, each option has advantages and challenges. Understanding these funding types will help you make the best decisions for *your* startup and set the foundation for your fundraising strategy.

STORYTELLING

ORGANIZATION

OUTREACH

CLOSING

Storytelling

A compelling narrative is at the heart of any successful fundraising campaign. Your story should highlight your vision, mission, and the problem your startup is solving. A well-crafted narrative aims to engage your potential investors but should also differentiate you from the competition. It's your chance to *showcase your passion, dedication, and the unique value proposition of your business.*

Organization

Preparing Your Content List
Your content list should include all the materials needed for a compelling pitch. This typically includes your pitch deck, executive summary, and financial projections. Each piece of content should be meticulously prepared and clearly present your business model, market opportunity, growth strategy, and financial health.

Organizing Your Data Room
A well-organized data room is vital for due diligence. It should contain all the necessary documents that investors will need to evaluate your startup thoroughly. This includes legal documents, financial statements, intellectual property information, and other relevant data. A transparent and accessible data room builds trust and facilitates a smooth due diligence process.

Term Sheets and Cap Tables
Understanding and negotiating term sheets is a critical aspect of the fundraising process. Nothing is "fair," but a clear and market-based term sheet sets the stage for a healthy investor relationship. Additionally, maintaining a clean and transparent cap table is essential. This ensures that ownership stakes are clearly defined and understood by all parties, preventing future disputes, and fostering investor confidence.

Outreach

Building Your Investor List

Creating a targeted list of potential investors is crucial. This includes *identifying investors aligned with your industry, growth stage, and funding needs.* A well-researched investor list increases the likelihood of finding the right partners who can provide not only the capital but also the strategic support, guidance, and valuable connections.

Researching Investors

Thorough research on each potential investor is essential. Understand their investment history, portfolio companies, and areas of interest. Tailor your pitch to strike a chord with their specific interests and demonstrate how your startup aligns with their investment thesis. Creating a more personalized approach significantly enhances your chances of securing funding.

Negotiating

Negotiation skills are vital when finalizing terms with investors. *It's important to balance securing the necessary capital and maintaining favorable terms for your startup.* Effective negotiation involves clear communication, understanding the investor's perspective, and being prepared to compromise on certain aspects while holding firm on others.

Closing

The closing list encompasses all the tasks and communications required to finalize the deal. This involves providing investors with clear instructions, following up with reminders, and ensuring all necessary paperwork is completed accurately. *Effective communication throughout this process is crucial* to getting caught off guard by situations that could have been avoided and ensuring a smooth closing.

Implementing the Funding Framework

To implement this comprehensive framework, start by assessing your current fundraising status and identifying any gaps in your strategy. Use the elements outlined in this book as a checklist to ensure you have covered all bases. Each framework component is designed to work in a structured approach to raising capital.

Remember, successful fundraising is not just about securing funds for your startup. It's about building lasting relationships with investors who share your vision and can contribute to your startup's growth.

Of course, it's not all roses. Things might not go as planned. Jonathan Charles of Samsung Catalyst acknowledges, "There is no shame in closing your startup after being intellectually honest with yourself and team given current difficulties in raising and then building a billion dollar plus company. You can always 'train' in a different, better-funded startup or inside a big tech company that embraces innovation. Often, just 'pivoting' into a white-hot sector will not work out. Train now on someone else's dime, and the time to get back into your own startup will come!"

While there's no perfect process for fundraising, I'm confident that you'll be well-equipped to navigate the fundraising landscape, close deals with confidence, and set your startup on a path to long-term success with these principles. You'll never know where your startup business will take you as you apply them, but I have watched companies grow to unicorn status from humble beginnings. Meanwhile, don't forget about your own team. Elizabeth Yin writes in *Raise Millions*, "Share with your team the plans on how your new funds will impact the company's runway and strategy. Remind the team to stay scrappy because fundraising successfully in the future is not always guaranteed."

As you move forward in your fundraising journey, continue to refine your approach, learn from each fundraising round, and adapt to the evolving market dynamics. Remember that the journey of building a successful startup is challenging but immensely rewarding. With the right strategy, persistence, and a clear vision, you can confidently achieve your fundraising goals. Good luck!

Glossary of Terms

Accredited Investor: High-net-worth individual based on SEC definitions of income and net worth.

Angel Investors: An angel investor is an accredited investor who invests their own money into a startup company in exchange for a portion of ownership. They typically provide funding in the early stages of a business's development.

Burn Rate: The amount a company is spending from its existing capital to fund operations before generating positive cash flow.

Capital Stack: The quantity of capital in various securities in a company and their relative seniority in a liquidation (in order of claims to the business and its assets). Senior Debt has the senior most claim and Common Stock is at the bottom (also known as the preference stack).

Cap Table (Capitalization Table): A formal spreadsheet or table that shows the capitalization for a company and by whom. It lists all company securities, such as common equity shares, preferred equity shares, warrants (rights to purchase shares), and who owns them. This is sometimes shown on a fully diluted basis, so imagine as though all securities are converted into common stock.

Convertible Note: A form of short-term debt that converts into equity, typically at the moment of a future financing round; essentially, the investor loans money to a startup, and instead of a return in the form of principal plus interest, the liability would convert into equity in the company, typically at a previous agreed upon price or a discount to what new investors are paying.

Dilution: The reduction in existing shareholders' ownership percentages of a business as a result of the company issuing new equity.

Drag-Along Rights: A clause in an agreement that enables a majority shareholder to force a minority shareholder to join in the sale of a company. The majority owner doing the dragging must give the minority shareholder the same price, terms, and conditions as any other seller.

Due Diligence: The investigation or exercise of care that a reasonable business or person is expected to take before entering into an agreement or contract with another party or an act with a certain standard of care. It involves verifying the material facts and figures presented by a startup during the funding process.

Equity: Ownership interest in a company, usually in the form of stock (varies classes of shares in the business), which represents a claim on the company's assets and earnings. This is usually comprised of common stock (ordinary) and preferred stock (more senior with special rights and liquidation preferences). Founders usually have only common stock.

Exit Strategy: A planned approach to exiting a venture, typically aimed at realizing a profit for the investors. Common exit strategies for startups include mergers and acquisitions (M&A), initial public offerings (IPO), or selling to a private investor such as a private equity firm.

FOMO (Fear of Missing Out): FOMO is the feeling of anxiety or unease that someone might miss out on something exciting or interesting happening elsewhere.

Participating Preferred Stock: A type of preferred stock that provides investors with a right to receive their original investment back and also participate in the distribution of the remaining proceeds with the common shareholders, if any, usually after a liquidity event like a sale of the company.

Seed Investing: Seed investing, also called seed funding or seed capital, is the first stage of funding for a startup. It's usually provided by angel investors or venture capital firms in exchange for a piece of the company.

Series A Funding:
- A priced round at a specific valuation that involves selling preferred stock to investors who believe in the company's potential for long-term success.

- Investors are looking for companies with viable business models and clear strategies for profitability.

- Series A funding sets the stage for transitioning from early development to more substantial operations

Series B Funding:
- Series B funding occurs after a startup has proven its viability and success through Series A funding with funds being used to scale the business

- Key players in Series B funding include venture capital firms specializing in later-stage investments.

Series C Funding:
- Series C funding is reserved for highly successful businesses seeking additional capital to further scale their operations.

- Companies at this stage look to develop additional products and new channels, enter new markets, or pursue strategic acquisitions.

- Companies engaging in Series C funding should have recurring revenue streams, established customer bases, and a track record of growth.

Serviceable Attainable Market (SAM): The size of the TAM you can practically target as you start selling your product.

Serviceable Obtainable Market (SOM): The SAM you can likely convert to your customers or users.

Silicon Valley: Silicon Valley is a famous place that now refers to much of the San Francisco Bay Area and is known for inventing many new technologies. It's home to lots of big tech companies like Google and Apple. The area got its name from the material used in computer chips, as Silicon Valley was home to many such companies in the area around Stanford University.

Startup: A startup is a new business just beginning its operations but with the expectation to grow exponentially in size and scale compared to a typical small or medium-sized business.

Term Sheet: A non-binding agreement establishing the basic terms and conditions under which an investment will be made. It serves as a template to develop more detailed legally binding documents.

Total Addressable Market (TAM): All the users in your entire market (often worldwide) multiplied by total annual sales per user.

VC (Venture Capitalist): A VC is an investor who gives money to new or growing companies in exchange for a share of ownership in the company. They often invest in startups or small businesses with the potential for high growth. They typically invest on behalf of the limited partners in their funds.

Pre-Money and Post-Money Valuation: Pre-money valuation refers to the value of the company before new financing or investment. Post-money valuation is the value of the company after the investment has been made. This is calculated by adding the amount of new equity to the pre-money valuation.

SAFE (Simple Agreement for Future Equity): An agreement between an investor and a company that provides rights to the investor for future equity in the company without determining a specific price per share at the time of the initial investment.

Lead Investor: An investor who organizes a venture capital round and typically contributes the largest amount of capital to the deal. The lead investor often plays a pivotal role in setting the terms of the investment and may also take a seat on the company's board of directors.

Liquidity Event: An event that allows the investors in a company to cash out some or all of their equity, such as a public offering or an acquisition.

Runway: The amount of time a company can continue to operate before it needs more financing or goes out of business. It's typically calculated by dividing the company's current cash balance by its monthly burn rate or negative cash flow.

Syndicate: A group of investors who come together to jointly fund a venture. Syndication allows investors to spread risk and invest in larger deals than they could handle individually.

Valuation Cap: In the context of convertible notes or SAFEs, a valuation cap is the maximum price at which an investor's investment will convert into equity during a future financing round. This is similar to the strike price of a call option. It is not and should not be viewed as the value of the business. That is likely not known, and these notes and SAFEs are known as unpriced rounds. It protects the investor by ensuring that their investment converts into equity at a reasonable price, even if the company's valuation increases quickly and much higher than the level of the cap.

Vesting: The process by which an employee earns rights to stock options or other forms of equity compensation over time. Vesting schedules are designed to incentivize employees to stay with the company for a longer period.

Additional Resources

Cooley: Legal Documents
https://www.cooleygo.com/documents/

The Great CEO Within: The Tactical Guide to Company Building, Matt Mochary, Mochary Films, 2019

Hustle Fund: Terminology
https://www.hustlefund.vc/post/vc-terminology

NVCA: Legal Documents
https://nvca.org/model-legal-documents/

Open VC: Startup Glossary
https://openvc.app/blog/startup-glossary

Raise Millions, Elizabeth Yin, Hustle Fund
https://letsgo.hustlefund.vc/raise-millions

Venture Deals: Be Smarter Than Your Lawyer and Venture Capitalist, 4th Edition, Brad Feld and Jason Mendelson, Wiley, 2019

Willson Sonsini: Legal Documents
https://ecvc.wsgr.com/

Y-Combinator: Term Sheets
https://www.ycombinator.com/library/4P-a-standard-and-clean-series-a-term-sheet

Want to check your knowledge from The Funding Framework?

Scan the **QR Code** below for insider insights and tips on Fundraising, Sales, Team–Building, and Scaling from **Startup System by Vijay Rajendran**

To learn about how to work with Vijay Rajendran and for our free **Knowledge Base Q&A**, featuring worksheets, and checklists on **https://www.mystartupsystem.com/knowledgebase**

If you are a startup, aspiring founder, or someone interested in fundraising, discover how we can collaborate by exploring *How We Can Work Together* at **Startup System**.

About the Author

Vijay Rajendran is an innovative leader and technology investor with a history of advising global companies, coaching startups, developing new markets, and creating new products and services.

Currently an advisor and executive coach to CEOs of startup companies, Vijay is the former head of Portfolio Value at 500 Global, a venture capital firm that invests early in founders building fast-growing technology companies. He led a global team helping startups and their founders develop connections, raise capital, and create a thriving community.

Vijay has been an innovation advisor and strategic partner to a wide range of industries, from financial services to retail to automotive. Previously, he was head of corporate innovation and partnerships at 500 Global, developing incubators and corporate accelerators for founders around the world and advising corporate venture capital teams. Before working in venture capital, he developed partnerships with fintech startups and worked directly with Entrepreneurs-in-Residence at global bank BBVA in San Francisco. As head of venture design, Vijay led a new Fintech ventures team and started one of the first digital banks for small businesses: Azlo. Additionally, he was a product innovation advisor with Jump Associates and a management consultant with Kearney, where he was a member of the Global Business Policy Council, a strategic service for CEOs. He also founded the gourmet e-commerce company Hungry Globetrotter.

Vijay grew up in five different countries. His passion for entrepreneurship has always been international: He was a Peace Corps technical advisor in Cameroon, working in microfinance. Vijay received a BS in Business Administration from Boston University, an MS in Foreign Service, and an MBA from Georgetown University. He is also an alumnus of the Berkeley Executive Coaching Institute at the University of California, Berkeley.

Vijay is the co-author of *The Secrets to Venture Studio Model Success, Unlocking Corporate Venture Capital*, and *Corporate-Startup Experiments* from 500 Global. He has led roundtables and workshops and spoken at conferences, including CB Insights Future of Fintech, Geneva Wealthtech Forum, Horasis Global Meeting, RISE, TiE IDEAS, and the Asia Financial Forum.

He lives with his wife and two daughters outside San Francisco, where he enjoys the good food, strong coffee, and stunning outdoors of the Bay Area.

www.ingramcontent.com/pod-product-compliance
Lightning Source LLC
Chambersburg PA
CBHW071707210326
41597CB00017B/2372